THE BATTLE OF
WATERLOO

THE BATTLE OF
WATERLOO

PETER & DAN SNOW

NATIONAL
ARMY
MUSEUM

ANDRE
DEUTSCH

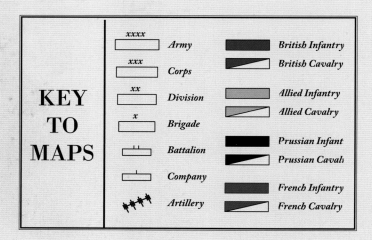

KEY TO MAPS

xxxx — Army	British Infantry
xxx — Corps	British Cavalry
xx — Division	Allied Infantry
x — Brigade	Allied Cavalry
Battalion	Prussian Infant
Company	Prussian Cavalr
Artillery	French Infantry
	French Cavalry

THIS IS AN ANDRÉ DEUTSCH BOOK

Published in 2017 by André Deutsch
An imprint of the Carlton Publishing Group
20 Mortimer Street
London W1T 3JW

10 9 8 7 6 5 4 3 2 1

Text © Peter & Dan Snow, 2015
Design and maps © André Deutsch, 2015, 2017

A CIP catalogue record for this book is available from the British Library.

ISBN978 0 233 00513 3

The content of this book first appeared in *The Battle of Waterloo Experience*, published by André Deutsch in 2015, ISBN 978 0 233 00447 1.

Printed in China

Front cover: Robert Gibb *Closing the Gates at Hougoumont*, 1815.

Page 2: *The Battle of Waterloo* by Sir William Allan (1782-1850).

Overleaf: *Waterloo*, 1815 by W H Sullivan, RCA (1870-1908).

CONTENTS

INTRODUCTION

WATERLOO CAN RIGHTLY CLAIM TO BE ONE of the greatest battles of all time. It was the battle that ended two decades of Europe's bloodiest conflict so far – the struggle to deny one of history's most formidable military geniuses complete domination of the continent. It was the final clash between the French Emperor Napoleon Bonaparte and a coalition of allies determined to get rid of him once and for all.

It was a battle whose outcome remained in the balance until the very end. For nine hours massed formations of infantry and cavalry on either side fought to break each other's resistance. For a moment the army that finally won looked near collapse. In all parts of the battlefield the contest was desperately close and the cost in human life was devastating. At least 45,000 men lay dead or wounded on the field when the battle was over. Europe paid a high price to end the Napoleonic wars.

But Waterloo bequeathed to Europe a century of relative peace. After the turmoil of the eighteenth century its states could turn their attention to the industrial and democratic revolutions of the nineteenth.

In this book we tell the story of what we believe is one of the most dramatic and captivating of military encounters. It was the climax of a lightning campaign by Napoleon to pre-empt an overwhelming offensive by his opponents. He began it brilliantly, catching the Prussians, divided from their British and other allies, and forcing both into an early retreat. But he was up against two military commanders who could match him in experience and determination. Marshal Blücher, the Prussian, was to lose no time in driving his defeated army to return to the struggle and join Wellington's mixed force of British, Germans and Dutch Belgians. It was to be the first time that Arthur Wellesley, Duke of Wellington, confronted Napoleon, but he had proved himself another of the world's greatest soldiers by his victories in India and his six year campaign to throw the French out of Spain and Portugal in which he never lost a

battle. Wellington brought all the skills he had learned in the Peninsular War into his first and final encounter with the French Emperor.

We will be examining the strengths and weaknesses of the three leaders and the nature of the armies and weapons they had under their command. This was the last continent-wide war fought with the musket, cannon and sabres. Little had changed from the days of Blenheim and Malplaquet a hundred years earlier. By the next great war in 1914 weaponry and communications were dramatically different. Wellington and Napoleon had to rely on men trained to carry out meticulous battlefield drills and on orders delivered on pieces of paper or by word of mouth.

Finally, like all the greatest battles, Waterloo is steeped in controversy. It ended in decisive victory, but it might so easily have turned out differently. Who made mistakes? Whose victory really was it? Would Wellington have won without Blücher? What was the main cause of the French defeat? We hope that this book will help answer some of these questions as well as recounting the story of this most fascinating of battles.

PETER & DAN SNOW

BACKGROUND

TO CONTEMPORARIES, THE PERIOD of conflict that followed the 1789 French Revolution was known as the "Great War". For decades, Europe and the world beyond were torn apart by discord. The scale and intensity of the fighting was unprecedented. During the revolution, France had flung off centuries of absolutist, monarchical rule amid bloody violence and civil war. The other nations of Europe had tried to intervene. But France had executed its king and queen, and its soldiers – fired with patriotic nationalism – had smashed the invaders. France then began a campaign to extend its newly found liberties to fellow citizens in neighbouring states. This was a war of peoples, of ideas and of identity.

At first, France fought Prussia and the sprawling Austrian empire. By 1793, Britain, Holland, Spain and Portugal were also at war. Instead of crushing the upstart French republic with its untested, divided leadership and its lack of old-regime generals, the powers of Europe found themselves defeated. They were humiliated by France's energetic and passionate new army, which fought with a shocking zeal, and whose leaders were chosen on merit and not by birth. Prussia withdrew its forces beyond the Rhine, while French troops pushed into northern Spain, captured Holland, and swatted aside British attempts to gain a foothold in France and support the regime's enemies. During one of these expeditions, when the British briefly held the vital naval base of Toulon on the Mediterranean coast, a young French artilleryman emerged as a dynamic and resourceful leader. This

24-year-old was destined to become one of the greatest commanders the world has ever seen: he was Napoleon Bonaparte.

Fresh from success in Toulon, Napoleon saved the revolutionary government from one of the many violent spasms that frequently gripped the streets of Paris. His carefully positioned artillery sent the mob scurrying. A grateful leadership presented him with the army of Italy. Napoleon now had the independent command that would allow his talents room to shine.

Over the following 20 years, Napoleon won countless victories on the fields of battle and in the corridors of power. After campaigns in Italy and Egypt, he returned home to seize political power. From November 1799, he ruled as a de facto dictator. As is so often the case, the turmoil, instability and anarchy of revolution had delivered a country – that had hoped to free itself from tyranny – into the hands of an absolute ruler more powerful than the kings he had replaced. In 1804, a reluctant Pope Pius VII was dragged from Rome to preside over a spectacular ceremony in which Napoleon crowned himself with the imperial crown.

The emperor went on to topple ancient empires, reshape France and redraw the map of Europe. His own ambition for ever-wider conquests made an implacable and unbending enemy out of Britain. France's island neighbour had long been its most bitter rival. Indeed, it was the French king's obsession with finally defeating the Royal Navy at sea that had bankrupted his regime and precipitated the slide to revolution. France and Britain (England before 1707)

Right: The storming of the Bastille, a castle in the heart of Paris which represented French royal power. It fell to a mob on 14 July 1789. This was the start of the Revolution and its capture remains the iconic expression of resistance to tyranny.

had fought no less than five wars in the space of 100 years, but the Revolutionary and Napoleonic wars were to be a mighty climax in which nothing less than global domination was the prize. Napoleon's plans for Europe were unacceptable to Britain. The British wished to see a balance of power on the Continent with important Channel ports and bases such as Malta, which British ships used for trade and to communicate with its empire, in neutral or friendly hands. Britain naturally saw no conflict between its

desire to restrain France in Europe and its own impulse to seize markets, resources and territory in Africa and Asia.

The resolute opposition of the British ultimately doomed Napoleon. Cut off from the world's trade by British naval blockades, he was forced to prey on France's neighbours to fill his coffers. Napoleon attempted to cut off the European market to British merchants by closing his ports to British ships. But as is the way with all prohibitions, this one led to rampant

Overleaf: The Battle of Rivoli, 14 January 1797. The 27-year-old Napoleon Bonaparte shocks the Austrians during a campaign that will see him force Austria to sue for peace and establish his reputation as one of history's greatest commanders.

NAPOLEON

1769–1821

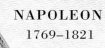

Napoleon was born in Corsica. Well-educated and trained as an artilleryman, he fought against the enemies of the French Revolution in the 1790s. His brilliance as a military commander during campaigns in the Mediterranean led him to seize power from the bankrupt revolutionary leaders in 1799. As First Consul and then from 1804 as Emperor of France, Napoleon made it his mission to spread what he saw as the benefits of the French Revolution throughout a Europe that was still steeped in feudalism. This led him to face several coalitions of European powers – all of which he soundly defeated until 1812. However, his disastrous Russian campaign in that year and his defeat by the Sixth Coalition at the 1813 Battle of Leipzig caused him to abdicate in April 1814. Napoleon was exiled to Elba but escaped and returned to Paris in March 1815. After his final defeat at Waterloo on 18 June 1815, he was exiled to the British island of St Helena where he died. He was married twice – to Josephine de Beauharnais until 1810 and then to Marie Louise, daughter of the Austrian emperor.

corruption and violence as Napoleon had to intervene to force allied governments to enforce his trade embargo with Britain.

Napoleon won staggering victories. At Ulm and Austerlitz in 1805, he knocked the Austrians out of the war. The following year, it took him three weeks to destroy the once mighty Prussian army and capture Berlin. He then fought a costly campaign against the Russians before smashing them at Friedland on 14 June 1807. Napoleon had stripped Britain of her Continental allies, but the island nation was determined to fight on, alone.

Desperate to choke off the flow of trade that Britain depended upon, Napoleon invaded Spain and Portugal to enforce his embargo. This was the start of the Peninsular War, which soon became a grim guerrilla struggle. Hundreds of thousands of French troops were killed, wounded or went missing as Spanish partisans slit throats and ambushed columns. The British helped with money, arms, and an ever-larger army that was commanded by a young British general who had made his name in India. He was the aristocrat Sir Arthur Wellesley. Victories against French opponents in Spain would see him ennobled, first as Viscount Wellington, and finally as a duke.

In 1810, however, Wellington's success was far from certain. Napoleon's forces controlled most of Spain and Portugal, despite suffering huge losses at the hands of the bubbling insurgency. The Russian tsar, Alexander I, was now France's ally, and

ARTHUR WELLESLEY, 1ST DUKE OF WELLINGTON 1769–1852

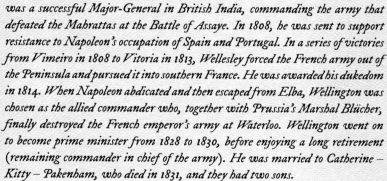

Wellesley was born to an Anglo-Irish family. He showed little promise during his early education in Dublin and later at Eton College, but he excelled at an equestrian school in France and joined the British army in 1787. He rose quickly through the ranks, and by 1803 was a successful Major-General in British India, commanding the army that defeated the Mahrattas at the Battle of Assaye. In 1808, he was sent to support resistance to Napoleon's occupation of Spain and Portugal. In a series of victories from Vimeiro in 1808 to Vitoria in 1813, Wellesley forced the French army out of the Peninsula and pursued it into southern France. He was awarded his dukedom in 1814. When Napoleon abdicated and then escaped from Elba, Wellington was chosen as the allied commander who, together with Prussia's Marshal Blücher, finally destroyed the French emperor's army at Waterloo. Wellington went on to become prime minister from 1828 to 1830, before enjoying a long retirement (remaining commander in chief of the army). He was married to Catherine – Kitty – Pakenham, who died in 1831, and they had two sons.

the Austrians had been defeated once again. Napoleon's siblings sat on thrones across Europe. From the walls of Gibraltar to the Skagerrak and from Brest to Ukraine, the Continent was utterly under the Napoleonic yoke. It was the most remarkable series of conquests in European history.

However, the success was short-lived. Within two years, Britain's continued opposition ensured that when tensions emerged between Europe's most powerful rulers, Napoleon and the Russian tsar, Alexander, the British were on hand offering incentives and whispering that Russia could never rest easy with a French tyrant dominating Europe. Russia was threatened by French support for a revived Poland – indeed, Russia's many Poles looked to such a revival with longing. Nor could Russia tolerate the debilitating effect on its trade that resulted from submitting to Napoleon's anti-British blockade. Alexander gradually reopened his ports to British ships, and, in 1812, Napoleon decided – as he had done so many times before – that conquest was the only sure way to have his orders obeyed.

Despite Wellington's success in the Peninsula (where 1812 would see him launch a brilliant invasion of Spain that threatened to destroy France's puppet regime), in June, Napoleon marched east and not south. On 23 June, a massive army of half a million men entered Russian territory and marched on Moscow. It was Napoleon's greatest gamble. The French hoped to live off the land, a tactic that had always allowed Napoleon to advance with astonishing speed. However, the Russians did not give them the chance. They retreated ever further into Russia, burning their own farms, driving away cattle and poisoning wells. Napoleon's troops either starved, were killed by partisans or deserted.

In September, the Russian army finally made a stand at Borodino and an indecisive bloodbath followed. The Russians retreated but were not broken, and Napoleon's battered and shrunken army staggered into Moscow. The city was empty and within hours was consumed by a terrible firestorm, either a deliberate ploy by the defenders or the product of chaotic looting by the French. Surrounded by ashes, bereft of food, and with the Russians refusing to negotiate or surrender, Napoleon began the long march back to friendly territory. He was beset by Cossack horsemen, guerrillas, and the winter cold; in November, after enduring unimaginable hardship, a mere 27,000 soldiers returned from Russian territory. One of history's greatest generals had just suffered one of the most legendary defeats.

There was an element of inevitability about the following two years. Europe rose, almost as one, against the weakened titan. Prussia, Russia, Sweden, Austria and other German states put over a million men into the field. Napoleon fought with his old brilliance against the often-ponderous coalition, but he was crushed at the mighty Battle of Leipzig in October 1813 and his dream of European mastery collapsed. In the spring of 1814, as Wellington advanced north from Spain, Napoleon fought superbly against the main allied juggernaut as it crossed the Rhine, headed for Paris. However, it was not enough to prevent the French capital falling in March. Napoleon bowed to reality and abdicated as emperor on 6 April. Europe sighed with relief: the Napoleonic Wars were over – or so it seemed.

Below: The Battle of Vittoria, 1813, by George Cruikshank. Wellington crushed Napoleon's brother Joseph at Vittoria on 21 June 1813 and conclusively brought an end to French rule in Spain. This satirical British take on the battle shows Joseph fleeing, Wellington striking a heroic pose and roast-beef-fed Britons routing their French enemy.

Overleaf: The Battle of Leipzig, 16–19 October 1813. Known as the Battle of Nations, it was one of the most decisive defeats suffered by Napoleon Bonaparte. Over half a million clashed in the biggest battle in Europe prior to the bloodbaths of World War One.

The Battle of Vittoria

THE HUNDRED DAYS

Left: Napoleon sets out from the island of Elba. This painting from c.1852 shows *L'Inconstant* and *Zéphir*. It was the start of one of the most desperate gambles in all European history.

NAPOLEON WAS TO RECEIVE surprisingly lenient treatment for a man that the allies blamed for long years of war. After his abdication and the restoration of the Bourbon dynasty to the throne of France in 1814, he was allowed to retire to the small island of Elba. There he busied himself with his miniscule empire, measuring just 28 km by 18 (17 miles by 11). He eagerly consumed reports from France as well as the news from Vienna, where his erstwhile enemies had gathered to redraw the map of Europe.

The news from France was full of promise for Napoleon. The new king did not command loyalty, let alone affection. The regime was shabby in its treatment of veterans of Napoleon's wars, and returning aristocrats sought revenge and restitution for crimes against loved ones and the loss of valuable property during the revolution. After the ruinous war, demobilized soldiers and the economy were suddenly recalibrating for the needs of peace, and economic conditions were harsh. Sullen groups of Napoleonic veterans met and drank to better

times. Crucially, Napoleon calculated that large numbers of French prisoners of war would be returning to France, giving him a readymade pool of troops to call upon if ever he was to seize back power. In Vienna, the allies appeared to be on the verge of declaring war on each other, as they wrestled with questions of territory and sovereignty. At one point, King Frederick William of Prussia even challenged the lead Austrian negotiator, Prince Metternich, to a duel.

While the leaders of old Europe bickered, Napoleon acted with his customary flair. In late February 1815, after less than 10 months in exile, he made a shockingly bold move. While the British representative on Elba, Sir Neil Campbell, was off in Tuscany visiting his mistress, Napoleon boarded a French brig disguised as a ship of the Royal Navy. On 1 March, accompanied by around 1,000 men, he landed in France on what is now some of the most fashionable real estate of the Côte d'Azur.

News that Napoleon had landed sped through France. A week later, with volunteers flocking to his banners, he was confronted with the first major royalist unit, outside Grenoble. He walked up to the enemy ranks, opened his jacket and roared, "Soldiers, if there is one among you who wishes to kill his emperor, he can do so. Here I am!" Not a shot was fired, but instead a chant of *"Vive l'Empereur!"* ("Long Live the Emperor") signalled the wholesale desertion of the unit to Napoleon. Grenoble fell without a fight, the first major city to do so. Napoleon later wrote, "Before Grenoble I was an adventurer; at Grenoble I was a ruling prince."

Napoleon's speed had always thrown his opponents and this time was no exception. He marched an average of 38 km (24 miles) a day. On 20 March, the day after the Bourbon court had fled north to Ghent (in today's Belgium), he was borne aloft by veterans as he arrived back at the Tuileries Palace in central Paris. In their haste to welcome their new sovereign, the staff had glued Napoleon's old insignia over the Bourbon fleurs-de-lis on the carpets.

Napoleon had judged the mood of France but not the mood of Europe. Disputes between the allies in Vienna were forgotten

Above: An idealized vision of Napoleon returning to his grateful people. Although artist Vasily Ivanovich Sternberg exaggerates, Napoleon was welcomed enthusiastically by many French civilians and the government forces sent to capture him.

GEBHARD LEBERECHT VON BLÜCHER
1742–1819

At 72, Prussian Field Marshal Blücher was the oldest of the top commanders at Waterloo. He started his military career at the age of 16 as a hussar in the Swedish army. When refused promotion because of his wild behaviour, he retired and took up farming for a time. Aggressive, brave and a shrewd strategist, Blücher joked that he was no intellect. His attitude to warfare was summed up by his nickname, "Marshal Forward". Blücher hated the French and loved the men under his command. He called them "my children" and, in return, they called him "Papa Blücher". In a letter to his wife the night after Waterloo, he wrote, "In conjunction with my friend Wellington, I put an end at once to Buonaparte's dancing. I had two horses killed under me."

as Napoleon's presence in Paris immediately galvanized them. He was declared an outlaw, and a treaty was forged that committed the great powers, once again, to rid Europe of Napoleon. Britain promised gold, men and Europe's best general, the Duke of Wellington. It was agreed that he would command an allied army in what is today Belgium, to operate in concert with a Prussian army under Marshal Blücher. The Austrians and Russians also rushed troops towards France, meaning that by the end of the 1815 campaigning season, the number of active coalition soldiers in a broad arc from northern Spain, through Italy and ending on the Channel coast, would be approaching one million men. A date was set for the invasion of France, 1 July.

Napoleon's only chance was to act decisively to defeat the elements of this mighty coalition in isolation before it could concentrate in overwhelming numbers. He set about calling his veterans back to their units and prepared for a pre-emptive strike. Over a period of two months, he took the 50,000 men of the Bourbon army and expanded it to around 200,000 ready to march, with a further 50,000 men in training. He found time to publish a new constitution, which extended the franchise further than that of King Louis that it replaced. The new constitution was put to a referendum in which the turnout was disappointing but the result was an unambiguous endorsement of Napoleon's settlement.

The obvious target for Napoleon's first strike was Wellington's allied army south west of Brussels, and its near neighbour, Blücher's Prussian army. They were the closest allied forces to the French border, the easiest to strike, and were likely to suffer from their divergent strategic interests. Wellington's lines of communication were to the Channel and the west; Blücher's ran in the opposite direction. An attack towards the hinge of their armies might force them to retreat

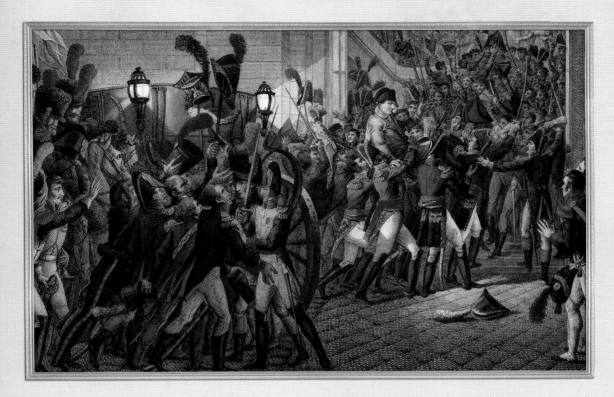

along their main supply routes, driving them apart. They could then be defeated, one after the other. Ultimately, this would also allow Napoleon the satisfaction of destroying his most intransigent enemy, the British army, commanded by the man – Wellington – who had made fools of French generals in Spain.

In early June 1815, Napoleon marched the 130,000-strong Army of the North up to the French border with what is now Belgium. They moved with stunning speed and in total secrecy. The frontier was sealed and no news of any sort was allowed to percolate through to the watchful Wellington. The British and Prussian armies were widely spread out across many hundreds of miles. Armies without modern logistics or canned food needed to remain thinly spread so as not to overload the food supplies of a particular area. Only when the moment of crisis arrived would they coalesce. The disadvantage of being on the defensive meant that they had to

remain spread out in order to cover the five different routes north that Napoleon could potentially take. Wellington and Blücher would take three days to concentrate their two forces and confront Napoleon together.

At 3.30am on 15 June 1815, French cavalry patrols crossed the southern border with the Kingdom of the Netherlands, into what is today Belgium. Napoleon was driving a wedge between the British and Prussian armies. Wellington did not hear about this until mid-afternoon, and like many British generals before and since, he immediately worried about his link with the Channel ports and home. Rather than rush to join with the Prussians, he ordered his men to watch for any threat from the southwest. Only that night, when reports reached him of a seemingly endless column of men approaching directly from the south, was Wellington convinced that this was Napoleon's main thrust.

When Wellington received this

Above: Napoleon is carried to the Tuileries Palace, 20 March 1815, hours after the French royal court made a dash for the border. Many of Napoleon's veterans were languishing out of work and were happy to see their hero return.

THE DUCHESS OF RICHMOND'S BALL
15 JUNE 1815

Novelists and poets have immortalized the Duchess of Richmond's Ball. "All Brussels had been in a state of excitement about it," wrote William Thackeray in Vanity Fair. *Lord Byron's poem "The Eve of Waterloo" opens with, "There was a sound of revelry by night", but soon "a deep sound strikes like a rising knell!" That sound, of course, is "the cannon's opening roar". The ball was actually held in a coachbuilder's house in a back street of Brussels, all the Duke and Duchess of Richmond could afford to rent. The duke had fallen on hard times when he overspent as Lord Lieutenant of Ireland. The duchess was particularly peeved that the Duke of Wellington called the house the "wash house" because it was in the Rue de la Blanchisserie – Laundry Street.*

confirmation, he was at a magnificent ball. It was thrown by the Duke of Richmond and, with the exception of a few generals, nearly every important officer in Wellington's army was there. Young officers danced with ladies with ever more urgency as rumours seeped between the guests and it became clear that the crisis was near. Many young men would rejoin their units and head into battle still wearing their dancing shoes.

Wellington rose from dinner and asked the Duke of Richmond for a map. The two dukes and some of their staff went into a private room where Wellington famously declared, "Napoleon has humbugged me, by God; he has gained 24 hours' march on me." He pointed to a crossroads called Quatre Bras where he had ordered his forces to concentrate, but added prophetically, "We shall not stop him there, and if so, I must fight him here." As he said "here", his thumb brushed the map at a point around 12 km (7 miles) north of Quatre Bras, near a village called Waterloo.

Right: Wellington and his British officers leave the Duchess of Richmond's ball in Brussels, heading south for Quatre Bras and Waterloo. Napoleon's brilliant dash north left the allies scrambling to respond. Some officers never changed out of their dancing clothes.

PROCLAMATION OF NAPOLEON

1 MARCH 1815

Frenchmen, the defection of the Duke of Castiglione delivered Lyon without defence to our enemies; the army, of which I had confided to him the command, was, by the number of its battalions, and the bravery and patriotism of the troops who composed it, in a condition to fight the Austrian army which was opposing it and to reach the rear of the left flank of the hostile army which was threatening Paris.

The victories of Champ-Aubert, Montmirail, Château-Thierry, Vauchamp, Mormans, Montereau, Craone, Reims, Arcy-sur-Aube and Saint-Dizier, the insurrection of the brave peasants of Lorraine, Champagne, Alsace, Franche-Comté and Bourgogne, and the position which I had taken at the rear of the hostile army, separating it from its magazines, its reserve parks, its convoys and all its equipment, had placed it in a desperate position. Frenchmen were never at the point of being more powerful, and the flower of the hostile army was lost beyond recovery; it would have found its grave in those vast countries which it had so pitilessly plundered, but that the treason of the Duke of Raguse gave up the capital and disorganized the army. The unexpected conduct of these two generals, who betrayed at one and the same time their fatherland, their prince and their benefactor, changed the destiny of the war. The disastrous situation of the enemy was such, that at the end of the affair which took place before Paris, they were without ammunition, through separation from their reserve parks.

Under these new and difficult circumstances my heart was torn, but my soul remained steadfast. I only thought of the interest of the fatherland; I exiled myself upon a rock in the midst of the sea; my life was and must still be useful to you. I did not allow the greater part of those who wished to accompany me to share my lot; I thought their presence was useful in France, and I only took with me a handful of valiant men as my guard.

Raised to the throne by your choice, everything that has been done without you is illegitimate. During the last twenty-five years, France has acquired new interests, new institutions, and a new glory, which can only be guaranteed by a national government and by a dynasty born under these new circumstances. A prince who should reign over you, who should be seated upon my throne by the power of the very armies who have devastated our territory, would seek in vain to support himself by the principles of feudal rights and he could only assure the honor and the rights of a small number of individuals, enemies of the people, who, for twenty-five years past, have condemned them in our national assemblies. Your internal peace and your foreign prestige would be forever lost.

Frenchmen! In my exile I have heard your complaints and your desires: you were claiming that government of your choice, which alone is legitimate. You were complaining of my long sleep, you reproached me with sacrificing to my own repose the great interests of the fatherland.

I have crossed the seas in the midst of perils of every sort; I arrive among you in order to reclaim my rights, which are yours. Everything which individuals have done, written or said since the taking of Paris, I will forever ignore; that will not in the least influence the recollection which I have of the important services that they have rendered; for there are events of such a nature that they are beyond human organization.

Frenchmen! There is no nation, however small it may be, which has not had the right to withdraw and which may not be withdrawn from the dishonor of obeying a prince imposed upon it by a momentarily victorious enemy. When Charles VII re-entered Paris and overthrew the ephemeral throne of Henry VI he recognized that he held his throne by the bravery of his soldiers and not from a prince regent of England.

It is therefore to you alone; and to the brave men of the army, that I consider and shall always consider it glorious to owe everything.

[Signed] NAPOLEON

PROCLAMATION.

Au Golfe-Juan, le 1.er Mars 1815.

NAPOLÉON,

Par la grace de Dieu et les Constitutions de l'État, Empereur des Français, *etc. etc. etc.*

AU PEUPLE FRANÇAIS.

FRANÇAIS,

La défection du duc de Castiglione livra Lyon sans défense à nos ennemis; l'armée dont je lui avais confié le commandement était, par le nombre de ses bataillons, la bravoure et le patriotisme des troupes qui la composaient, à même de battre le corps d'armée Autrichien qui lui était opposé, et d'arriver sur les derrières du flanc gauche de l'armée ennemie qui menaçait Paris.

Les victoires de Champ-Aubert, de Montmirail, de Château-Thierry, de Vauchamp, de Mormans, de Montereau, de Craone, de Reims, d'Arcy-sur-Aube et de saint-Dizier, l'insurrection des braves paysans de la Lorraine, de la Champagne, de l'Alsace, de la Franche-Comté et de la Bourgogne, et la position que j'avais prise sur les derrières de l'armée ennemie en la séparant de ses magasins, de ses parcs de réserve, de ses convois et de tous ses équipages, l'avaient placée dans une situation désespérée. Les Français ne furent jamais sur le point d'être plus puissans, et l'élite de l'armée ennemie était perdue sans ressource; elle eut trouvé son tombeau dans ces vastes contrées qu'elle avait si impitoyablement saccagées, lorsque la trahison du duc de Raguse livra la Capitale et désorganisa l'armée. La conduite inattendue de ces deux généraux qui trahirent à la fois leur patrie, leur prince et leur bienfaiteur, changea le destin de la guerre. La situation désastreuse de l'ennemi était telle, qu'à la fin de l'affaire qui eut lieu devant Paris, il était sans munitions, par la séparation de ses parcs de réserve.

Dans ces nouvelles et grandes circonstances, mon cœur fut déchiré: mais mon âme resta inébranlable. Je ne consultai que l'intérêt de la patrie: je m'exilai sur un rocher au milieu des mers; ma vie vous était et devait encore vous être utile, je ne permis pas que le grand nombre de citoyens qui voulaient m'accompagner partageassent mon sort; je crus leur présence utile à la France, et je n'emmenai avec moi qu'une poignée de braves, nécessaires à ma garde.

Elevé au Trône par votre choix, tout ce qui a été fait sans vous est illégitime. Depuis vingt-cinq ans la France a de nouveaux intérêts, de nouvelles institutions,

une nouvelle gloire qui ne peuvent être garantis que par un Gouvernement national et par une dynastie née dans ces nouvelles circonstances. Un prince qui régnerait sur vous, qui serait assis sur mon trône par la force des mêmes armées qui ont ravagé notre territoire, chercherait en vain à s'étayer des principes du droit féodal, il ne pourrait assurer l'honneur et les droits que d'un petit nombre d'individus ennemis du peuple qui depuis vingt-cinq ans les a condamnés dans toutes nos assemblées nationales. Votre tranquilité intérieure et votre considération extérieure seraient perdues à jamais.

Français! dans mon exil, j'ai entendu vos plaintes et vos vœux; vous réclamez ce Gouvernement de votre choix qui seul est légitime. Vous accusiez mon long sommeil, vous me reprochiez de sacrifier à mon repos les grands intérêts de la patrie,

J'ai traversé les mers au milieu des périls de toute espèce; j'arrive parmi vous, reprendre mes droits qui sont les vôtres. Tout ce que des individus ont fait, écrit ou dit depuis la prise de Paris, je l'ignorerai toujours; cela n'influera en rien sur le souvenir que je conserve des services importans qu'ils ont rendus, car il est des événemens d'une telle nature qu'ils sont au-dessus de l'organisation humaine.

Français! Il n'est aucune nation, quelque petite qu'elle soit, qui n'ait eu le droit et ne se soit soustraite au déshonneur d'obéir à un Prince imposé par un ennemi momentanément victorieux. Lorsque Charles VII rentra à Paris et renversa le trône éphémère de Henri VI, il reconnut tenir son trône de la vaillance de ses braves et non d'un prince régent d'Angleterre.

C'est aussi à vous seuls, et aux braves de l'armée, que je fais et ferai toujours gloire de tout devoir.

Signé NAPOLÉON.

Par l'Empereur:

Le grand maréchal faisant fonctions de Major-général de la Grande Armée.

signé, Comte BERTRAND.

 A VALENCIENNES, chez H. J. PRIGNET, Imprimeur des Administrations, etc. 1815.

NAPOLEON
AND
HIS ARMY

NAPOLEON'S ARMY AT WATERLOO was not the finely honed weapon that he had wielded in the Austerlitz campaign of 1805. In that year, he had spent the summer drilling his men to the point of exhaustion. Troops would have gone through the complex series of manoeuvres that warfare in this age of musket and cannon demanded as if they were second nature. Officers would have known the strengths and weaknesses of every one of their men.

Perhaps most important of all, Napoleon's senior commanders would have understood his thinking and the reasons behind his orders. His subordinate generals – or marshals as they were known in the French army – would have shared Napoleon's strategic vision and he could have trusted them to make decisions that meshed perfectly with his plan of operations. These were all powerful factors for his crowning success against the Austrian and Russian armies that year, but a decade later at Waterloo it would be the shortcomings in all these departments that meant Napoleon was unable to replicate his former glories.

Napoleon had also changed in himself. Although accounts differ, several witnesses noticed that there was something in their commander that burned less brightly. One of his staff officers Colonel Pétiet found that Napoleon could no longer spend long hours in the saddle. The man who had once scoured every fold in the landscape, visited every unit, and stayed awake all night dictating orders, now needed time to sit and rest. Pétiet wrote that Napoleon's "corpulence", his dull pallid complexion and his stiff gait made him seem "quite different from the General Bonaparte I had known at the beginning of my career." Napoleon was not the general he once had been.

Perhaps the French army's greatest weakness, though, was the shortage of quality among Napoleon's subordinate commanders. His marshals, once the band of brothers who had been the key to his success, were now

Right: Nicolas Soult, Duke of Dalmatia. He joined the French army as a private but rose rapidly to become one of Napoleon's best marshals. At Waterloo he took on the role of chief of staff. He was a pale reflection of Napoleon's legendary chief of staff Louis-Alexandre Berthier, who had refused to rejoin the Emperor.

Left: This print *Serrez les rangs* (close ranks) shows a grizzled veteran, a holder of the Legion d'Honneur, standing firm under enemy fire. He is encouraging the novices around him to close up or stay shoulder to shoulder as enemy fire kills and wounds their comrades. A sprinkling of gnarled veterans was seen as vital if a newly raised unit was to be battle-ready.

MICHEL NEY

1769–1815

Know as Le Rougeaud ("red faced"), Ney was bad-tempered, impetuous and a poor strategist, but he showed flair and courage that inspired his soldiers. In 1813, he was given the title, Prince of Moscow, for his leadership at the Battle of Borodino. Said to be the last Frenchman to leave Russian soil in the famous retreat of 1812, Napoleon called him "the bravest of the brave".

Five horses were shot under him at Waterloo; however, some say his failure to break the allied squares led to the French defeat. After Napoleon's exile, Ney was tried and found guilty of treason. Executed by a firing squad on 7 December, he refused to wear a blindfold. Permitted to give the order to fire, he said, "When I give the order, fire straight to my heart. Wait for the order. It will be my last to you."

either dead, dull or had defected. Masséna, one of Napoleon's best marshals, refused to rejoin his former commander and remained in retirement; likewise, Victor, Marmont and Oudinot too were unwilling. The brilliant Berthier, Napoleon's former chief of staff, declined to take up his old position, and died in a mysterious accident in June 1815. Mortier was ill, the brilliant Lannes was dead and Davout – who had smashed the main Prussian army at Jena-Auerstedt with a force half its size – was instructed to remain in Paris to keep the Emperor's unreliable capital loyal.

This last decision may well have cost Napoleon his empire. In place of these marshals, Napoleon promoted men who were far less capable. Soult was a decent soldier but a pale reflection of Berthier in the position of chief of staff. To command the left wing of his army, Napoleon chose the extraordinary Marshal Ney, nicknamed *le Brave des Braves* ("the bravest of the brave") by the Emperor himself for his almost superhuman courage and exposure to risk on the battlefield. He was a superb leader of men in the thick of battle but his grasp of strategy would prove terribly lacking. An equally bizarre appointment was that of Napoleon's most junior marshal, Grouchy, to command the right wing. Grouchy had never commanded an independent corps before, and in the critical days of mid-June 1815, it showed.

Most of the officers in Napoleon's army were veterans of one or more of the Emperor's campaigns. The army was almost entirely French, and political opponents had been purged from the ranks. Around 75 per cent of the officers had been promoted the hard way. Former private soldiers, they had risen through the ranks and had gained reputations on the battlefield. They owed the Emperor a fanatical loyalty for their enhanced professional and social status. However, like Napoleon, these true believers were no longer young. The men in their late twenties and early thirties who had once

Below: The Battle of Montmirail, 11 February 1814. Here the veterans of the French Old Guard attack and swing the battle for the Emperor. It is a striking impression of the impact that a disciplined mass of veterans can have at the critical point of a battle.

EMMANUEL DE GROUCHY
1766–1847

Grouchy's father, the 1st Marquis de Grouchy, was rumoured to be the illegitimate son of King Louis XV but an aristocratic upbringing did not stop him from becoming an enthusiastic supporter of the French Revolution. Marshal Grouchy's distinguished military career was overshadowed by his failure to turn up at Waterloo. "Inspiration in war is only appropriate to the commander in chief," he wrote. "Lieutenants must confine themselves to executing orders." He insisted Napoleon had not ordered him back to Waterloo. Napoleon disagreed and blamed "Grouchy's imbecility" for his defeat. After the battle, Grouchy was exiled and lived in the United States until permitted to return to France in 1821. He died aged 81.

rampaged across Europe were now firmly middle aged.

The soldiers these officers commanded were also veterans. The class of conscripts for 1815 had not yet been through training, so nearly every man had served in at least one campaign. Many were youngsters who knew only the desperate struggle of 1814, but there were sizeable numbers of men who had followed Napoleon from Spain to the Russian Steppe. In some ways, it was a great army full of hardened volunteers, motivated and committed to the Emperor's cause. In other ways, though, it was fragile. Units of veterans can be harder to control, are less likely to obey orders blindly and are quick to look to their own salvation if the situation appears to be irretrievable. As ever, Napoleon the adventurer and the risk taker, needed momentum and victories if he was to ensure his army remained intact and dedicated.

An infantryman needed all the resolution possible if he was to fight and win a battle during this period. The weapons technology available meant that armies often found themselves standing no more than a few metres apart, blasting each other

with primitive guns (called muskets), the effective range of which was about 100 metres (328 feet). When one side broke and fled, the victor would set about the fugitives with the razor-sharp 50-cm (20-inch) blade on the end of his musket known as a bayonet. Every man needed to be able to fire approximately three shots a minute, and it took an experienced soldier about 20 seconds to reload. This slow rate of fire meant that men stood in dense masses less than 1 metre (3 feet) apart from their neighbours, and two or more ranks deep. The effect of all these individuals firing together would be to send a heavy storm of musket balls hurtling towards the enemy.

Training was required to accustom the men to standing still and firing like automatons while around them their comrades fell wounded or killed. It was also vital to get the men to and from the battlefield in good order, and then deploy them facing in the right direction to allow them to bring massed musket fire on their enemy. Moving several hundred 20-year-olds across rough country when each was armed with a long musket and bayonet, in the close order required to

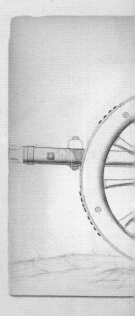

achieve these massed volleys, was extremely challenging. Endless drilling was needed to move the men from the files – in which they marched along roads – into the columns that the French liked to attack in, about 40 men wide and 15 men deep. If cavalry was present, it could quickly get around the flanks and rear of a column; then the men had to perform another manoeuvre, smoothly forming a hollow square to allow 360-degree defence. The speed at which infantry could perform all these manoeuvres would determine the course of a battle. The column had one major weakness: the men in the ranks behind the front could not easily bring their weapons to bear on an enemy facing them. Time and again in the Peninsular War, the British – deployed in long lines where each man had an open field of fire – worked havoc on the attacking French columns.

Also prominent on the battlefield were the cavalry. As well as performing reconnaissance roles, they were a shock weapon and could appear rapidly with thundering impact. The cavalry were particularly adept at breaking the will of an already shaky enemy, and could cover large distances to act as a rapid-reaction force and plug a gap that had appeared in their own side's lines. Glamorous,

magnificently attired, and brave to a fault, the cavalry were a stunning but deeply unreliable weapon. Napoleon's hussars, light cavalrymen who prided themselves on their recklessness, boasted that they would not live to see their thirtieth birthdays.

Napoleon himself began as an artilleryman. "God," he liked to say, "fights on the side with the best artillery." He had an unshakeable faith in cannon, fielding an imposing 250 at Waterloo. These could fire heavy iron shot or explosive rounds at troops over 1 km (0.6 miles) away. Napoleon liked his guns to be light, so they could be quickly limbered up to horses and redeployed on the battlefield to support an attack. The cooperation between infantry, cavalry and artillery had been a lethal combination on countless battlefields.

In all, Napoleon would have approximately 48,000 infantry and 14,000 cavalry for his attack on Wellington on the morning of the Battle of Waterloo. They would be supported by 7,000 artillerymen manning around 250 guns. The numbers were roughly equal to those of the allied army opposite, although Napoleon was armed with more cannon. If the Prussians managed to link up with Wellington, however, Napoleon and his army would be dangerously outnumbered.

Below: A 12-pounder field gun. These guns could be very mobile as teams of horses galloped them around the battlefield. Napoleon was first and foremost a gunner. "It is with cannon", he once wrote, "that one makes war."

THE ALLIED COMMANDERS AND THEIR ARMY

THE FORCES ARRAYED AGAINST Napoleon Bonaparte were confusingly diverse as befitted a rainbow coalition of the European states. Field Marshal Blücher's Prussian army was a fascinating mix. Prussia's defeats at the hands of Napoleon had forced it into a radical reorganization. Compulsory military service had been introduced – at the end of their time in the army, conscripts were liable to be recalled to serve in reserve regiments. These lacked some of the qualities of full-time units but would prove just as reliable, particularly in defence. Officers were drawn from the land-owning classes: they were men with generations of service to the Prussian crown in their blood.

Blücher had seven regular regiments, 10 reserve regiments dressed in a patchwork of old uniforms, and five regiments from Prussia's new territories. These five had been acquired as the French empire in Germany collapsed, and some of them were still dressed in their old French uniforms. Blücher also had two regiments raised by the Russians that had been drawn from Germans and other nationalities who had become prisoners of war in the 1812–14 campaigns against Napoleon. Alongside these regular units, there were also over a dozen militia regiments, some packed with veterans and others with novices. All in all,

the Prussian army was extremely uneven in quality and not up to the standard of the great Prussian armies of the past.

Wellington commanded an even more unorthodox collection of units. Only a third of his army was from the United Kingdom. Over 60 per cent of his men came from the Duchies of Nassau and Brunswick, the electorate of Hanover, and the Dutch-Belgian Kingdom of the Netherlands. All of these nations had only just re-emerged as sovereign powers after being absorbed into Napoleon's sprawling empire. Their armies had barely been assembled. Many of the officers and men were experienced, but only because they had fought for Napoleon when their homelands had been part of his empire. At best, these units were completely untested; at worst, many of the men in them retained their loyalty to the Emperor for whom they had so recently been fighting. Alongside the regular battalions of the Dutch-Belgian Netherlands and some of the German states, there were also militia units. Just as was the case with the Prussian army, these militiamen tended to lack the commitment, training and equipment to be relied upon.

Wellington was all too aware of the weaknesses of his army. Although he had about 50,000 infantrymen – 2,000 more than Napoleon – over 12,000 of them were militiamen. He also had 11,000 cavalrymen, and 6,000 gunners manning 150 guns (100 guns fewer than the French). Around one third of Wellington's army was British, or rather from the United Kingdom. Even in the English regiments, up to a half of the men were Irish. Ireland, a land of large families and poor soil, provided a huge number of Wellington's officers too; these were men who lacked the commercial opportunities of neighbouring Britain, and who instead looked to make their fortunes with the sword.

The common soldiers were usually drawn from the very lowest rungs of society; they were men who had been waifs and strays from the docks, slums, prisons and hamlets. Although the Royal Navy was permitted to seize men forcibly through "impressment" and enlist them aboard ship, the army had to recruit its soldiers. Sergeants roamed the alleys and lanes painting a rosy picture of Indian riches and battlefield booty, and promising boys on the very margin of Georgian society an escape from a grinding existence. Cheap booze flowed and bounties were distributed, much of which would later be deducted for kit and expenses once the recruit had signed up – for life. Wellington said that the British army was recruited from "the scum of the earth". They enlisted, he claimed, "from having got bastard children – some for minor offences – many more for drink…" However, he concluded that it was "…wonderful that we should have made them the fine fellows they are."

The regiment was the basic unit of the British army. It was responsible for recruiting, equipping and training battalions of men, and sending them off to war. Some regiments recruited men from wherever they happened to be billeted, but this was a transitional period and many regiments were developing strong local associations. Perhaps the most famous of

Below: Wellington's Band of Brothers. From left to right they are: the Prince of Orange; the Duke of Brunswick (standing); the Duke of Wellington; General Lord Hill; General Sir Thomas Picton (seated); Marshal Blücher; and Lord Uxbridge. These men would determine the fate of the allied cause at Waterloo.

ROYAL ARTILLERY.

London Pub.d Feb.y 1.st 1813 by Colnaghi & Co. 23 Cockspur Street.

GRENADIERS of the XLII.d or ROYAL and XCII.d or
GORDON HIGHLANDERS.

London Pub.d Nov.r 1, 1812 for Colnaghi & Co. 23 Cockspur Street.

60.th Reg.t   95.th Reg.t

BRITISH RIFLEMEN.

London Pub.d May 16 1812 by Colnaghi & C.o 23 Cockspur Street.

A PRIVATE of the 7.th or QUEEN'S OWN L.D.(HUSSARS.)

London Pub.d Sep.r 1 1812 by Colnaghi & C.o 23 Cockspur Street.

HENRY PAGET
1768–1854

Handsome and well connected, Henry Paget inherited the title Earl of Uxbridge. A member of the British parliament, he raised a regiment of Staffordshire volunteers that took part in the Flanders Campaign of 1794. Joining the British army a year later, Uxbridge rose quickly through the ranks, distinguishing himself as a brave cavalry commander. His calm acceptance of the loss of his leg at Waterloo made Uxbridge a legend. Following the battle, he was created 1st Marquess of Anglesey. When the Duke of Wellington held his last Waterloo anniversary dinner in 1852, the crowd waiting outside his house gave Anglesey the loudest cheer.

these were the Highland regiments, which could be predominantly Gaelic-speaking and raised by a colonel who might also be the clan chief. They were essentially the ancestral clan war party, formalized and given red coats by the British government. They marched into battle wearing kilts and carrying broadswords, and to the sound of shrieking bagpipes. For 50 years, the Highlanders had been the shock troops of the British army, comprehensively shedding their former reputation as villainous rebels.

When well led, these Highlanders as well as other British soldiers certainly could fight. Under Wellington, the army in the Iberian Peninsula had won a stunning sequence of victories over Napoleon's marshals. The British General had driven the French entirely out of Spain and Portugal, and had even invaded southern France in the autumn of 1813 (long before any other allied power). Wellington had been the critical ingredient. He was sparing with his men's lives and they loved him for it. His choice of battlefield demonstrated a gift for reading a landscape. He countered the French preponderance in artillery by hiding his men behind hills and

slopes. He had an instinctive ability to be at the point of crisis and direct the deployment of reserves himself.

Wellington exuded a calm assurance born from his experience in dozens of battles. He knew that if his units could meet the French onslaught in long ordered lines, as little as two men deep, their musket volleys would shatter the French assault no matter how imposing or terrifying it might appear. He infuriated bean counters by insisting that his men train with live powder and shot. While bureaucrats regarded this as an expensive waste, it certainly ensured that by the end of the Napoleonic wars, the British army was renowned for standing like rock and firing volley after volley in perfect order.

In front of the solid line of infantrymen was a screen of skirmishers. The men of the famous green-jacketed 95th Rifle Regiment were brilliant practitioners of this kind of warfare. They were trained to fight in open order, not in ranks, and they used more accurate Baker rifles to harass the enemy and shoot individual enemy commanders. The rifle had an effective range of up to 300 metres (984 feet), compared to the musket's

Opposite: Engravings from *Costumes of the Army of the British Empire According to the Last Regulations,* 1812, by Charles Hamilton Smith. Clockwise from top left: Royal Artillery; Grenadiers of the 42nd (or Royal) and 92nd or Gordon Highlanders; A Private of the 7th or Queen's Own Hussars - Lord Uxbridge's own regiment; British riflemen of the 60th (standing) and 95th (kneeling) regiments.

range of well under 100 metres (328 feet). Frustratingly for Wellington, five companies of riflemen had been sent to America in 1814, but the remaining units were rushed back into service and would play a central role on the field of Waterloo.

Wellington's cavalry gave him cause for concern. A magnificent weapon, the cavalry was also a deeply unreliable one. The duke's cavalry commander was Henry Paget, Earl of Uxbridge, who had conducted a long affair with Wellington's brother's wife. Wellington therefore resisted Uxbridge's appointment, but was forced to accept him by the army chief of staff in London, the Duke of York. Wellington also doubted Uxbridge's suitability to exercise command over a cavalry that had proved ungovernable at the best of times.

Wellington had a clear disadvantage in artillery. He had around 150 cannon, a full hundred fewer than Napoleon. Wellington knew that the French would seek to batter his army into a pulp, dishearten the untested and rapidly mobilized units, and then drive a mass of infantry at them to finish the job. Wellington needed cannon to cut down swathes of French infantry when the attacks came.

Overall, Wellington lacked the hardened infantry, the practised cavalry and the weight of guns to be confident of success. He described his army as "an infamous army, very weak and ill-equipped". He may have been trying to dampen expectations as he approached his first and only battle with Napoleon, one of history's greatest commanders. But Wellington was not entirely exaggerating.

Right: Recruiting for King George's army. Recruiting sergeants travelled the length of Britain and Ireland coaxing young men and boys to enlist. The navy were allowed to forcibly impress, but the army had to rely on a rough wooing. Alcohol was freely distributed, drums and fifes were played, tales of riches and adventures were disseminated. Few recruits had any inkling of the brutal life a British redcoat faced on campaign.

In the mean time Sir Wm Delancey will carry
on the duties of the Department — & from the little I
have seen of him, I make no doubt but we shall
proceed with a perfect good understanding —

I have had the happiness of hearing very lately from
Mrs Nicolay, that she & the children were well —

I am greatly struck with the richness of this
Country, which is cultivated to a degree really astonishing — In this town there is a considerable mag-
nificence in the style of the buildings — & the rides &
walks in the neighbourhood are very fine — I should
however for a residence give the preference to Ghent
or some of the places of less note than Bruxelles —
Indeed the only fault in Ghent is the total want
of variety in the ground which is perfectly flat —
but otherwise the town is extremely neat & clean, &
the neighbourhood beautiful for a flat country —

From Ostend to Ghent, we travelled entirely by water
there being either part of the River or an artificial Canal,

A letter of 17 May 1815 from Lieutenant-Colonel William Nicolay of the Royal Staff Corps to Major-General John Brown, speculating who will be appointed the Duke of Wellington's Quartermaster-General. He goes on to detail, as the Royal Staff Crops was tasked to do, the quality of the roads that the British Army will have to negotiate in the coming Waterloo campaign.

"The cross roads are bad, being quite sandy soil, & a little of our Hythe Shingle would be very desirable – On this account all the principal Roads are paved in the middle for use in bad weather – with another road at each side, for dry weather, which answers therefore very well – and almost universally there are rows of trees on both sides of the roads…"

LIEUTENANT
STANDISH O'GRADY

30 MAY 1815

Lieutenant Standish O'Grady of the 7th Hussars, writes to his father as "Lord Chief Baron" (he was an Irish judge) on 30 May 1815. He described the previous day's troop review in the fields opposite the village of Schendelbeke:

> "…all the British cavalry and the horse artillery were inspected by the Duke of Wellington the day before yesterday there never was so fine a sight… Old Blucher said he never saw such a sight in his life and valued the horses at 3 million of money, he said he should shut himself up when he went back to the Prussians for three days to endeavor to forget how inferior they were to us – Lord Wellington said that the 10th Hussars were the most beautiful horses he ever saw… to which Lord Uxbridge added in his short way 'Damn it the 7th can't be improved they are perfect'. It was really beautiful to see Lord Uxbridge manuvering [sic] 46 squadrons on ground that could but just hold them but he can do it in capital style – I have dined with him sometimes and like him much he is quite familiar as one of ourselves."

<table>
</table>

Damn it they 7th cant be improved they
are perfect— It was really beautiful to
see a Hythridge manoeuvring 46 Squadrons
on ground that could but just hold
them but he can do it in capital Style—
I have dined with him sometimes and like
him much he is quite as familiar as one
of ourselves & be we to quit Vivians Brigade
and he brigaded with the 15th under Sir Colquhoun
Grant he is a very fine fellow I believe as
brave as a lion and rather a good fellow
Tho' the 10th never could act under him—I
have to thank you for my glass which an
Officer of the 15th told me he had for me.
the report here is that we advance
shortly but not to act very offensively
as that honor is to be conferred on the
Russians & Prussians and our first duty is
merely as a corps of observation I hope
it will not last long as I should not
wish the miseries of a Campaigne and
none of its comforts which is always the
case in these half & half measures—the
Germans desert in the front and we
are to send a Bgd to relieve them I suppose
the 10th the most likely in order to display
2 ventures valor which I shall ever doubt,
and am certain, at least that it will
not be volunteered I sincerely hope

LIGNY AND QUATRE BRAS

BY 11PM ON THE NIGHT OF 15 JUNE, the scene at the Duchess of Richmond's ball was pandemonium. Napoleon's army was poised to strike and the race was suddenly on to confront him. It was not a moment too soon.

All through the early evening, Wellington had been determined to preserve as calm a demeanour as possible. He had been coolly receiving messages detailing the strengths and locations of the advancing French army. Napoleon's men attacked and seized Charleroi at 5am. Wellington claimed that he didn't hear about this until the evening. Some doubters say he must have heard earlier and that he was slow to react. It is, after all, only 48 km (30 miles) from Charleroi to Brussels, a three-hour horseback ride. But that first message didn't tell Wellington what he really wanted to know – where Napoleon's main army was located. If the Charleroi attack was a feint to distract from a far more powerful thrust from the southwest through Mons, then he would have to move his troops in a quite different direction. It wasn't until late at night that he heard that there was no sign of an attack through Mons. The French were advancing straight up from the south and pressing the Prussians back to the town of Sombreffe. Immediately, Wellington ordered his officers at the ball to instruct their units to move off and head due south.

The spot they headed for was Quatre Bras – the "Four Arms" crossroads – nearly 32 km (20 miles) south. That was where Wellington

Below: A contemporary, if stylized, painting of the death of Duke Frederick William of Brunswick at Quatre Bras.

THE PRELUDE TO WATERLOO
15–17 JUNE 1815

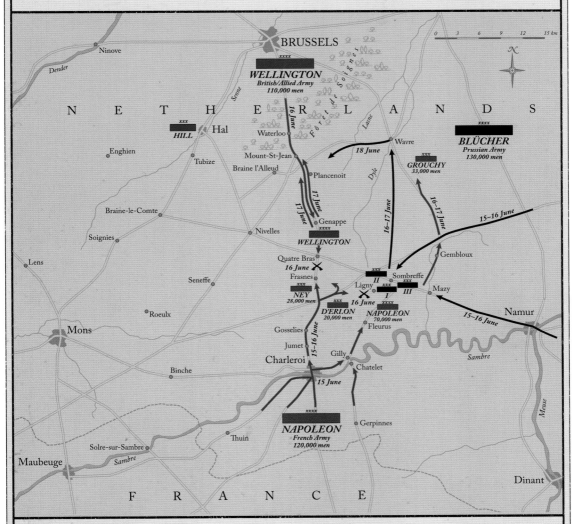

AT 5 AM ON 15 JUNE the French army crosses the Sambre at Charleroi and throws back an advance guard of the Prussian army. Napoleon splits his forces leading the bulk of his army to meet Marshal Blücher's Prussians and sends a smaller force under Marshal Ney to head up the direct road towards Brussels. Three of Blücher's four corps gather around Sombreffe, while Wellington waits in Brussels to be sure that Napoleon isn't approaching from Mons to the southwest.

On the 16th, the French attack and defeat the Prussians at Ligny and force them to retreat to Wavre pursued by Marshal Grouchy. Wellington rushes what troops he has available to the crossroads at Quatre Bras to block Ney. Ney is unable to break through and d'Erlon's corps, in a confusion of orders, proves unable to help either Ney or Napoleon.

On the 17th, Wellington, hearing that Blücher has withdrawn, pulls back his forces to the ridge of Mont St Jean just south of Waterloo. Napoleon is slow to follow up in heavy rain. By the morning of the 18th, most of his men and guns are struggling through the mud to take up position to attack Wellington. Blücher, beaten but not broken, promises to come to Wellington's aid.

would make his stand. He arrived there at 10am – there was no sign of the enemy. The Dutch Belgians would hold the position until Wellington's other troops arrived. The duke reckoned he had time to ride the 12 km (7 miles) east to where Blücher was preparing to meet the advancing French.

Napoleon's plans were going well. He knew he had enough troops to destroy only one allied army at a time. The small Prussian force at Charleroi had been scattered and Blücher's main force was now in sight. There was no sign of Wellington. Napoleon would attack and eliminate Blücher before turning on Wellington. This involved leading the bulk of his army to smash the Prussians at Sombreffe and sending Marshal Ney with around 28,000 men to secure the crossroads at Quatre Bras. With the Prussians defeated, only Wellington would stand between him and Brussels.

Wellington found the Prussians forming columns in open country near Ligny and quietly told an aide that he feared they were inviting heavy bombardment by Napoleon's artillery and probable defeat in battle. When Wellington met Blücher, he came under pressure – particularly from the Prussian chief of staff General Gneisenau – to detach part of his army to reinforce the Prussians. Wellington replied that he would move his army to help provided he was not attacked himself. It was as well that he made this provision, because when he returned to Quatre Bras it was immediately clear that he would have a struggle to hold the crossroads against the building attack from Marshal Ney's force.

Wellington discovered the Dutch-Belgians retreating in disorder from the woods and fields south of the crossroads, and but for the arrival of Sir Thomas Picton's division, he would have been powerless to prevent Ney seizing this key junction. Picton, a cantankerous Welshman wearing a great wide-brimmed civilian hat, was one of Wellington's best and most experienced generals. He and many of the men in his division had been in the forefront of battles that Wellington had won against the French in the Peninsula. Now they would take the brunt of Ney's assault on the crossroads of Quatre Bras.

Above: Elizabeth Southerden Thompson, Lady Butler painted this striking imagining of Quatre Bras in 1875. The tenacity of British infantry forming squares to resist the courageous French cavalry attacks was a feature of Quatre Bras and, famously, of Waterloo itself.

AUGUST NEIDHARDT GRAF VON GNEISENAU
1760–1831

Lieutenant General Gneisenau called his army's pursuit of the French after Waterloo "the most glorious night of my life". Dour, suspicious but a brilliant strategist, Gneisenau was a perfect counterpoint to Blücher. The son of an impoverished Saxon solider, he began his military career in the Austrian army. He travelled across the Atlantic in support of the British during the American Revolution, and went on to transform the Prussian army. Between 1807 and 1813, he led moves to abolish corporal punishment and promote soldiers on merit, and set up military academies. During the twentieth century, two German battleships and a post-war frigate were named after him.

Picton drew up his men in long lines to give every musket a clear field of fire – a technique that had proved devastatingly effective in the Peninsula. Wellington's lines of infantry had destroyed attacking French columns at Vimeiro, Bussaco and Fuentes de Onoro. And they did it again under the command of the formidable Thomas Picton at Quatre Bras. However, Ney was able to deploy one fearsome force of Frenchmen that few, if any, of the British Peninsular veterans had ever seen before. They were the cavalrymen known as the cuirassiers. And they came close to winning the battle of Quatre Bras for Napoleon.

During most of the battle of Quatre Bras, Wellington's Anglo-Allied force had no cavalry to support the hard-pressed infantry. They were still struggling to negotiate the packed roads from their assembly points several miles away. This meant that Ney's heavy cavalry had the ground to themselves, and wherever they found vulnerable units of infantry they wreaked havoc. The only way Wellington's men could resist the charges of the *cuirassiers* was to form squares, each side bristling with bayonets four ranks deep, to frighten off the attacking horses. But the confusion of the melee, and the orders and counter orders to shift from line to square and back again, meant that regiments were sometimes exposed to the French cavalry. When they were, the carnage was near catastrophic. One regiment, the 69th from South Lincolnshire, was badly cut to pieces. Survivors raced for shelter to a nearby square that had managed to hold together against persistent attacks. Ney was also able to push forward his *tirailleurs*, skirmishers who, in the absence of Wellington's cavalry, were able to come close enough to pick off large numbers of his infantry.

Wellington himself was constantly in the heat of the battle, riding up and down the line tirelessly shouting encouragement and shifting units when gaps appeared in the line. At one point, chased by French hussars and lancers, he had to call on a defensive line of Highlanders to duck their heads and lower their bayonets so that he could spur his horse to leap over them and seek shelter.

The fierce fighting at Quatre Bras went on for six hours, and only when more units began to fill his ranks was Wellington able to move forward. By early evening, he had turned the tables on Ney, who was now seriously outnumbered, and the French were pushed back. The allies and the French each lost some 4,500 killed and wounded. Ney also suffered from the extraordinary

mishandling of Count d'Erlon's corps. D'Erlon was ordered to take his 20,000 men to reinforce Ney. But just as they were about to join Ney at Quatre Bras – where they might have been decisive in swaying the battle in his favour – Napoleon ordered them urgently back to join him in his battle with the Prussians at Ligny. Then, just as d'Erlon was about to join Napoleon to deliver what could have been a knockout blow to the Prussians, Ney summoned d'Erlon back again to Quatre Bras. In the end, a quarter of Napoleon's army played no part in either battle. It was the first major blunder of the French Emperor's campaign.

The battle Napoleon fought with Blücher at the village of Ligny was as fierce a struggle as the battle of Quatre Bras. After his artillery had dealt massive damage to the Prussians, Napoleon advanced on a wide front. The French were able to force the Prussians to conduct a fighting withdrawal

back through the village of Ligny and beyond. But Ney, who was supposed to have blocked Wellington and then turned east to help Napoleon, was nowhere to be seen, and d'Erlon was engaged in his futile march and countermarch. What should have been a crushing defeat for the Prussians became a damaging but not crippling reverse. Their 72-year-old commander, Marshal Blücher, who was thrown from his horse as he led a charge, was out of action in the immediate aftermath of the battle. The question now was whether the wisest course for the Prussians was to stay, ready to support Wellington, or to leave the field altogether. After all, some argued, Wellington had failed to help them at Ligny. But once Blücher recovered from his fall and was back in the saddle later that evening, he threw his weight behind those in high command who favoured staying close to Wellington. He was single-mindedly determined to destroy Napoleon,

Above: "Prince Blucher under his horse..." The Prussian commander was badly beaten up when he fell from his horse at Ligny. It took impressive personal willpower for him to stay focused on the wider strategic situation. His decision, hours after his fall, to march towards Wellington was probably the most important of the entire campaign.

and to hold what was left of his army ready to go to Wellington's rescue when Napoleon turned against him.

The Prussians withdrew to Wavre and Napoleon sent Marshal Grouchy in pursuit. On the morning of the 17th, Wellington learned that the Prussians were retreating. In order to avoid being outflanked by Napoleon, he ordered his army to withdraw to a ridge halfway back on the road to Brussels that he had carefully reconnoitered months earlier. It was called Mont St Jean, just south of a small village called Waterloo.

Napoleon was slow to move. He failed to press hard on the heels of either Wellington or the Prussians, and both armies were able to withdraw in reasonable order. That night, 17 June, the heavens opened. Soaked to the skin, the Anglo-Allied army took up position on the ridge under Wellington's direction on ground that soon became a sea of mud.

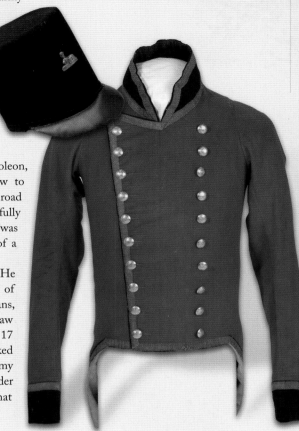

Far left: A "Shako" or cap worn by an officer of the 92nd (Highland) Regiment of Foot at the time of Waterloo. The badge featuring the Sphinx evokes the unit's service in Egypt, where its men, although terribly reduced in number by disease and enemy action, begged to be allowed to return to the fray. The regiment also served Wellington with great distinction through most of his Peninsular campaign.

Left: This "coatee" or coat was worn by Lieutenant Colonel William Miller of the elite 1st Foot Guards in 1815. Nearly all British infantrymen wore scarlet coats, but different regiments would have different colour "facings". Here they are blue.

THOMAS PICTON
1758–1815

Wellington described Picton as "a rough foul-mouthed devil", but added that "no man could do better in different services I assigned him". A cantankerous and controversial figure, Picton was found guilty in 1806 of condoning the torture of a 14-year-old mulatto girl (suspected of stealing) while he was Governor of Trinidad. The conviction was later overturned. In 1810, Wellington requested that Picton join his command in the Peninsular War. Picton's so-called "fighting" 3rd Division was key to Wellington's victories at Badajoz and Vittoria. Before the Battle of Waterloo, Picton confided to an aide-de-camp that he had a premonition that he would never return to his native Wales. He was the most senior British officer to die on the battlefield.

Below: Charge of the 1st Life Guards at Genape 17 June 1815 by Richard Simkin.

"I take this opportunity of addressing you with a few lines which I hope will find you in Good Health as this leaves me at this Period. I suppose you must have heard of A Battle that has Been Fought by this. I assure you it was A Bloody one and any Person that were in it never could expect to come out of it Alive seeing there Comrades fall on each side of them at such A Tremendous Rate I for my own Part thought of nothing But Fighting and Gaining the victory and it Pleas'd the all mighty to grant my Request and keep me from being Injured thanks be to him for his Preservation[.] on Saturday the 17th of June we marched A very heavy Day s march after Fighting nearly all the Day before[.] we lay in A Been Field that night and it Rained in Torrents we all being so Fatieug'd we were forc'd to lay Down and in less than an Hour we were almost Drown'd in water and in that condition lay'd all night[.] in the Morning about 8 oClock we saw the French on A Hill in Front we were on one hill and they on another they advanc'd our Cannon Play'd on them they [advanced] towards A wood by A Farm house [Hougoumont] as soon as the General saw there intentions the Brigade of Guards were sent there imediately we came into the wood when it began very sharp in less than 3 Hours we could hardly go along for Dead Bodies we Charg'd them and Drove them But in less than an ½ Hour we were forced to retreat into an apple orchard where [we] remained in Breast works some small time being reinforc'd by A small Party of German Legions [elements of Colonel Charles du Plat's King's German Legion brigade] we again Charg'd them and drove them and afterwards kep our Position until about 7 oClock in the Evening when Wellington perceived there Right Gave way we again Chard'd them and they Ran in all Directions we follow'd them as long as we Could see and after we halted the Prussians had Came up they Follow'd Killed and took Prisoners A Great amount we hear there were taken 30000 Prisoners and upwards of 200 Peices of Cannon I cannot say any thing Perticular more Concerning it so I hope and trust you will make yourself Happy on my account as I am in hopes all things are nearly setled and I have not the least Dowt But Peace will once more be restord to our native Isle and I may say to all [E]urope. I hope my little Daughter is in Good Health and all the Family."

James July 12th 1815

Dear Wife

I take this oportunity of addressing you in
these lines which I hope will find you in good health
this leaves me at this period I suppose you must
have heard of A battle that has been fought by
this — I asure you it was A bloody one and any
Person that were in it scarcd could expect A comming
of it Alive seeing their comanders fall on each
side of them at such A trumendious rate & for
my own Part thought of nothing but fighting
and Gaining the Victory and it Pleasd the all
mighty to grant my Request and keep me from
being Injured thanks be to him for his Preservation
on Saturday the 17th of June we Marched A very heavy
Days March after fighting nearly all the Day before
we lay in A Deenfield by night and it raind on
us in torrents we all being so fatigud we were forcd to
lay Down and in less than an Hour we were
almost Drownd in water and in that condition
layd all night in the Morning about 8 oClock
we saw the French on A hill in front
of we were on one hill and they on another they
advancd our Cannon Playd on them they however
shered by A farm house as soon as the general

THE BATTLE BEGINS: THE FIGHT FOR HOUGOUMONT

SUNDAY MORNING – 18 JUNE – dawned warm and sunny. Few men on either side had escaped the ravages of the night's downpour. Most had slept in the open, struggling to contrive any shelter for themselves and for their arms and equipment. Now they had their first clear sight of the battlefield that would decide the future of Europe.

Wellington had spread his forces along a shallow ridge about 3 km (2 miles) long. A sunken road ran along the top, and the ground in front sloped gently down to a valley. Beyond it – about a kilometre away, where the ground rose again – Napoleon's troops were gathering. Many were still moving up the main road from Charleroi to Brussels that cut through the centre of both armies. Brussels, Napoleon's objective, was just 16

Below: Wellington retreats from Quatre Bras to Waterloo. The British army is portrayed as in good spirits as it trudges north in retreat. Wellington was confident that the ridge he had reconnoitred at Mont St Jean would offer the best chance to stop Napoleon before Brussels.

JEROME BONAPARTE
1784–1860

Napoleon scoffed when Jerome reported a waiter had overheard Wellington saying the Prussians were on their way to support him on the eve of Waterloo. He had every reason to distrust his notoriously unreliable youngest brother. Over the years, Napoleon had annulled Jerome's marriage to an American, was scandalized by his extravagance as King of Westphalia, and was infuriated when Jerome abandoned the Russian campaign after being criticized for travelling in ostentatious luxury. He did not redeem himself at Waterloo, spending the entire battle unsuccessfully trying to take Hougoumont. Jerome died of a stroke aged 76 while gambling at cards.

km (10 miles) away. He didn't appear to be in a hurry. The sodden ground made it difficult to drag his big guns forward into a line from where they could bombard Wellington's ridge. His strategy was a simple one: once the ground was dry enough, and his troops and guns were assembled, his artillery would pound Wellington's ridge and open the way for his massed infantry to break through – as they had in many battles with the Austrians, Prussians and Russians.

However, this was the first time Napoleon had faced Wellington, and the British general had chosen his ground carefully. The ridge of Mont St Jean sloped away on the north side too; this was where Wellington placed nearly all his units, the allied infantry hidden just behind the brow and the cavalry further back. The French could see only a Dutch-Belgian brigade on the slope facing them, and a scattering of light infantry skirmishers.

Wellington's strategic planning went further. He made strongpoints of three buildings on the forward slope. They jutted

out like fortified breakwaters designed to spoil the clean sweep of any mass French assault. Facing Napoleon's right was the farm of Papelotte, in the centre the strongly built farm compound of La Haye Sainte, and way over on the left – on Wellington's right and partly hidden in trees – the farm of Hougoumont. The last two were to play critical roles in the battle.

Napoleon was suffering from some physical discomfort. He was no longer the fit young commander he had been at Austerlitz 10 years earlier, but he was confident of victory. He rode up and down the French lines prompting enthusiastic cries of *"Vive L'Empereur!"* British outposts could see him clearly moving along the brightly coloured ranks of the infantry, and the blaze of blue, green and red tunics and glinting breastplates of the cavalry. Napoleon had 72,000 men in the field. Another 30,000 under Marshal Grouchy had been despatched to harass the Prussians who had been trounced at Ligny. The French

Above: A telescope from 1815. This was a vital tool but one which officers would have to pay for themselves. With AGW engraved on it, this belonged to Colonel Alexander George Woodford of the 3rd Regiment of Foot Guards.

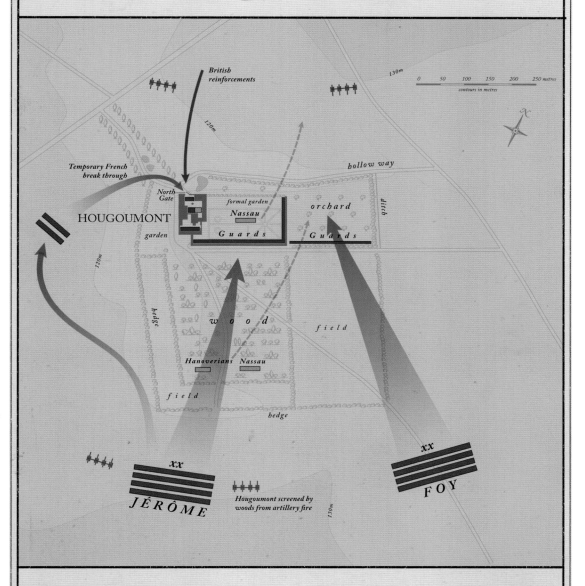

THE **BATTLE** FOR **HOUGOUMONT**
ALL DAY, 18 JUNE 1815

—2—

British reinforcements

130m

0   50   100   150   200   250 metres

contours in metres

120m

Temporary French break through

hollow way

North Gate

HOUGOUMONT

formal garden

Nassau

orchard

garden

Guards

Guards

ditch

120m

hedge

w o o d

field

Hanoverians Nassau

field

hedge

xx

JÉRÔME

Hougoumont screened by woods from artillery fire

130m

xx

FOY

THE BATTLE FOR THE FARMHOUSE and its garden and orchard rages all day. Wellington's Nassau battalion fails to hold the wood to the south of the farm. The British guardsmen are forced back into the farm buildings and the garden, and at one stage the French break through the north gate. They are repelled and the gate is closed. The initial British detachments are reinforced by Scots and Coldstream guardsmen and manage to hold off the French assaults by Jérôme and Foy throughout the day.

emperor knew that Blücher and his men were in and around Wavre, less than 16 km (10 miles) away, but believed they would now be too weak to help Wellington. With his eyes on the road to Brussels, Napoleon ordered his infantry to prepare to advance against the ridge ahead: d'Erlon's corps – eager to make up for the fiasco of the 16th – would be on the right, Reille's corps on the left. Behind them were the cavalry of Milhaud and Kellerman, and in reserve the Imperial Guard.

At a breakfast meeting, Napoleon breezily told his commanders they would be in Brussels that night. Some of them urged caution: Reille and d'Erlon, who had faced Wellington in the Peninsula, recalled the formidable fighting power of his infantry in defence. Nicolas Soult, who had been defeated by Wellington at Oporto in 1809 and in the Pyrenees and southern France in 1813 and 1814, begged Napoleon to recall Grouchy immediately.

The Emperor refused, replying that Wellington was "a bad general" and the English were "bad troops". Then he declared, "This affair is nothing more serious than eating one's breakfast." Soult is said to have muttered, "I earnestly hope so."

Wellington deployed his main force on the reverse slope behind the ridge with Thomas Picton's mostly British battalions at his left centre and the Guards on his right. Among and between them, Wellington

Above: The Morning of the Battle of Waterloo by Ernest Crofts. While Napoleon and his marshals ate a fine breakfast and discussed Wellington's likely tactics, the men outside shook off the night's cold and wet.

placed the units of his Dutch and German allies, hoping that they would be inspired by the prowess of the British veterans on either side of them. For his own part, Wellington had been heartened by a message from Blücher promising to put up to 50,000 Prussian troops on the road to Waterloo at dawn. If they arrived in time, they should help give Wellington the victory.

The old farmhouse of Hougoumont and its garden was to be the most fiercely contested spot on the battlefield. Wellington chose to make it a keystone of his defence. As long as his troops could hold it, they would be able to blunt any attempt by Napoleon to roll up the allied army from the right. The British commander rode down to the farm early on Sunday morning and told the man in command, Lieutenant-Colonel James Macdonnell of the Coldstream Guards, that it must be held at all costs. Macdonnell, a giant Highlander from Invergarry, had 200 guardsmen and 1,000 Germans from Nassau under his command.

Napoleon's brother Prince Jerome Bonaparte commanded the infantry division facing the farm. He had none of the military flair of his brother and, no doubt aware of the need to impress, he threw one battalion after another into the fight. It was a massive challenge. The siege began at 11am and continued on and off for most of the day. The French, fighting desperately and with great valour, managed to push the Nassauers out of

Above: Napoleon giving orders to as aide-de-camp for Marshal Grouchy on the morning of 18 June 1815. The pivotal decision to send 30,000 men to pursue the Prussian army under Blücher has come under huge scrutiny ever since. Grouchy failed to stop the Prussians joining Wellington that afternoon and may have cost Napoleon the battle.

JAMES MACDONNELL

1781–1857

On the eve of Waterloo, Wellington sent Coldstream Guardsman Lieutenant-Colonel Macdonnell, to command the defence of Hougoumont. Macdonnell already had a distinguished Napoleonic war record fighting the French in the Peninsula and in the Mediterranean. When Wellington was told the farm was bound to fall into enemy hands, he responded, "You do not know Macdonnell." The brawny colonel proved his commander right when French soldiers broke through the double gate into Hougoumont's courtyard. There was hand-to-hand fighting with axes, swords and musket butts. Macdonnell, though wounded and with his face covered in blood, managed to force the gates closed. Wellington later called him "the bravest man in the British army".

the wood to the south of the farmhouse and from the orchard on its east side. Hundreds died on both sides, including the commander of Jerome's lead brigade. Macdonnell's guardsmen, struggling to defend the farm itself, were compelled to seek shelter inside the north gate of the compound. Sous-Lieutenant Legros, a towering Frenchman – known as *L'Enfonceur* (the Enforcer) – smashed through the gate with about 30 others and pandemonium followed. Macdonnell shouted for help to slam the gate shut. Somehow, he and half a dozen others managed it and Legros and his comrades, who were frantically fighting for their lives inside the farmyard, were surrounded and gradually cut down. The only one spared – a story has it – was a young French drummer boy.

Wellington now reinforced the defenders of Hougoumont with more Coldstream and Scots guardsmen, and a bloody shootout continued all day round the walls of the farm. Time and again, at huge cost, the French – with no fewer than 20 more battalions thrust into the fray by Jerome and another divisional commander General Maximilien Foy – attacked the garden wall protecting the compound. It was 2 metres (6¹/₂ feet) high and the British had knocked loopholes through it. This allowed the guardsmen to fire from behind the relative safety of the wall at wave after wave of charging Frenchmen. The French made

easy targets: the open space beyond the wall became known as the "killing ground" as bodies piled up in what by afternoon had become a hopeless struggle. Remarkably, Napoleon failed to give his assaulting infantry artillery support. It may have been hard to target Hougoumont, obscured as it was by trees from most directions, but the French emperor and his generals seemed to have made no effort to bring guns up to a spot where they might have shattered the walls and made its defence impossible. Only in the afternoon, did Napoleon order incendiaries to be fired into the compound. This caused the barn to catch fire but still left the outside walls standing.

The unsuccessful attempt to storm Hougoumont left 5,000 French dead and wounded, while the British and Nassauers lost fewer than a thousand. Moreover, the costly commitment of much of Reille's corps left it unable to do much to contribute to Napoleon's main thrust against Wellington's line. Hougoumont pinned down around a quarter of the emperor's entire infantry throughout the battle of Waterloo. Their failure to break in decisively and crush the farm's defenders – particularly as so many men had been expended in the attempt – was a tactical disaster. It's hardly surprising that Wellington later remarked, "The success of the Battle of Waterloo depended on the closing of the gates at Hougoumont."

Overleaf: Defence of the Chateau de Hougoumont by the flank company, Coldstream Guards, by Denis Dighton. Dighton made drawings soon after the battle in 1815, and his depiction is another reminder that as well as the long-range death from cannon fire, Waterloo was also a battle in which men were caught up in brutal, intimate battles at close quarters. The British troops (on the right), here fighting outside the south gate of Hougoumont, were eventually forced inside the farm, which they managed to defend successfully.

Left: Robert Gibb painted one of the most iconic images of Waterloo, *Closing the Gates at Hougoumont*, 1815, over a century later but it captures some of the gritty, hand-to-hand nature of the fighting in and around Hougoumont Chateau. When the British finally forced the gate shut, they were able to eliminate the 30 or so Frenchmen trapped inside.

BATTLE OF
WATERLOO MAP

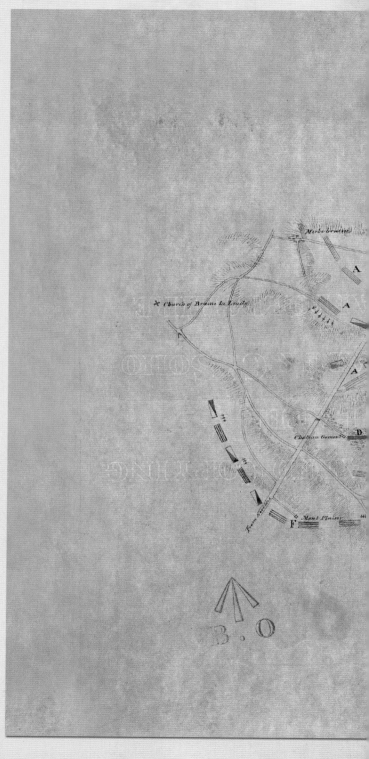

A sketch of the ground and dispositions for the Battle of Waterloo, drawn by Captain Thompson and Lieutenant Gilbert of the Royal Engineers. The two men describe the Chateau at Hougoumont and its surrounding trees as "the wood which the enemy endeavoured to gain but without success".

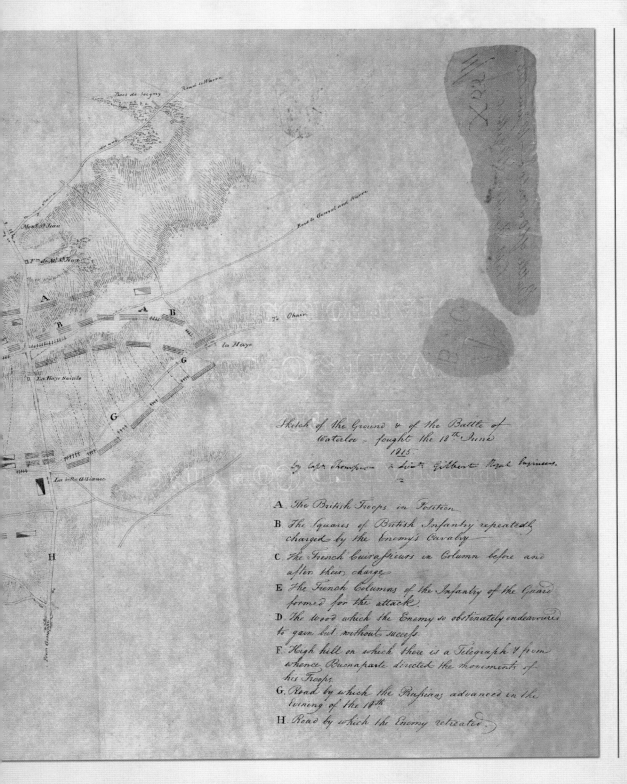

Sketch of the Ground & of the Battle of
Waterloo - fought the 18th June
1815.
by Capt. Thompson & Lieut. Gilbert Royal Engineers.

A. The British Troops in Position

B. The Squares of British Infantry repeatedly charged by the Enemy's Cavalry

C. The French Cuirassiers in Column before and after their charge

E. The French Columns of the Infantry of the Guard formed for the attack

D. The Wood which the Enemy so obstinately endeavoured to gain but without success.

F. High hill on which there is a Telegraph & from whence Buonaparte directed the movements of his Troops.

G. Road by which the Prussians advanced in the Evening of the 18th.

H. Road by which the Enemy retreated.

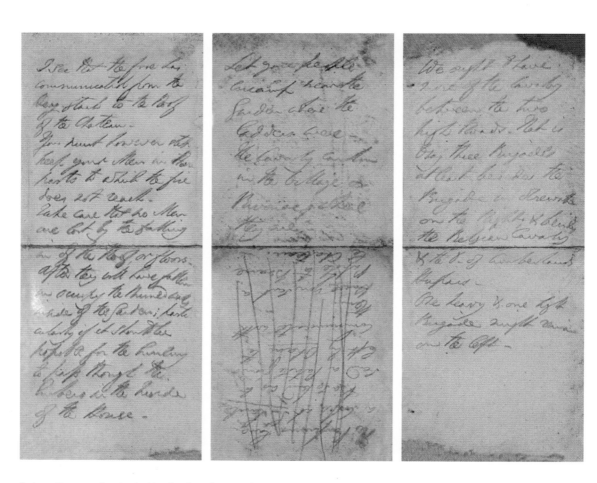

Strips of prepared animal skin, bearing the pencil-written orders in the Duke of Wellington's hand, to unit commanders fighting at Waterloo.

"I see that the fire has communicated from the hay stack to the Roof of the Chateau.

You must however still keep your Men in those parts to which the fire does not reach.

Take care that no Men are lost by the falling in of the Roof, or floors. After they will have fallen in occupy the Ruined walls inside of the Garden; particularly if it should be possible for the Enemy to pass through the Embers in the Inside of the House.

We ought to have some of the Cavalry between the two high Roads. That is to say three Brigades at least besides the Brigade in [indecipherable, most probably a place name] on the Right; & besides, the Belgian Calvary & the D[uke] of Cumberland's Hussars.

One heavy & one light Brigade might remain on the left.

Let you people encamp near the Garden where the ladders were. The Cavalry can stand in the village, or Bivouac where they are."

WATERLOO: THE BATTLEFRONTS
11AM, 18 JUNE 1815

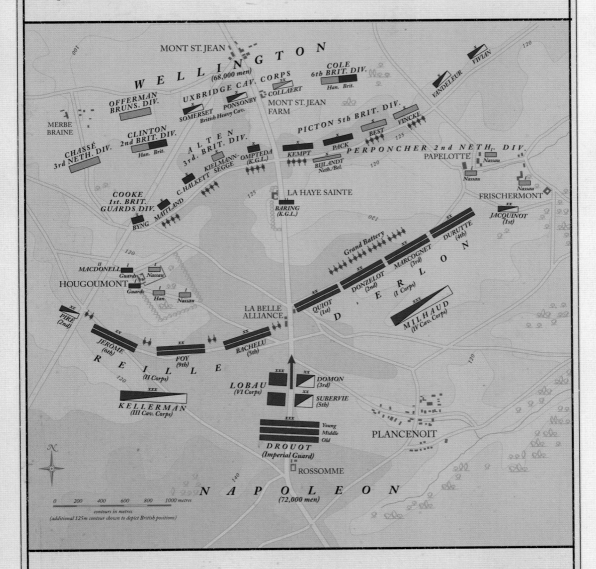

WELLINGTON DEPLOYS HIS MIXED ARMY OF BRITISH and allied troops just behind the ridge at Mont St Jean and the sunken road that runs along it. Only one Dutch-Belgian brigade is on the forward slope. Wellington places small detachments in front of his line at the key outposts of Hougoumont, La Haye Sainte and Papelotte. Napoleon spreads his forces out on the south side of a gentle valley between him and Wellington. His Grand Battery of guns takes most of the morning to move into position on his centre right.

D'ERLON'S INFANTRY ATTACK AND THE BRITISH CAVALRY CHARGE

THE FRENCH ATTACK ON Hougoumont was only intended to be a distraction while Napoleon prepared his main assault on the centre of Wellington's line. By 11am, the French Emperor finally had his big guns in place – 54 12- and 6-pounders in his so-called *Grande Batterie*, and another 18 horse artillery 6-pounders. They roared into action, firing 120 rounds a minute at Wellington's ridge. But the vast majority of the allied army, carefully placed behind the brow of the hill by Wellington, was invisible to the French gunners. Much of the heavy shot landed off target and the mud softened its impact.

The bombardment lasted more than two hours and Napoleon planned to follow it with a massed infantry attack. But he was in for a shock. At around 1pm, the Emperor spotted troops approaching well over to his right through woods 7 or 8 km (4 or 5 miles) away. At first he allowed himself to believe that they were Grouchy's men, but he soon learned that they were Prussians. To Napoleon's astonishment, Blücher had recovered sufficiently from his defeat at Ligny to send reinforcements to Wellington. Napoleon regretted not having ordered Grouchy to rejoin him earlier and promptly sent him an urgent message demanding his return. In addition, an immediate order was

sent to Count d'Erlon to set in motion his massed columns of around 20,000 infantry who were to break though Wellington's lines and open the road to Brussels.

Phase two of the battle of Waterloo had begun. An immense array of footsoldiers – each of d'Erlon's divisions in a huge column with one battalion behind the other – began what was to become a laborious tramp up the long slope to the ridge. The memory of Wellington's destruction of his

Below: The eagle captured by Sergeant Charles Ewart, 2nd Dragoons. It was the battle standard of the French 45th Line Infantry Regiment. Capturing an imperial eagle was the highest achievement imaginable, resulting in instant promotion.

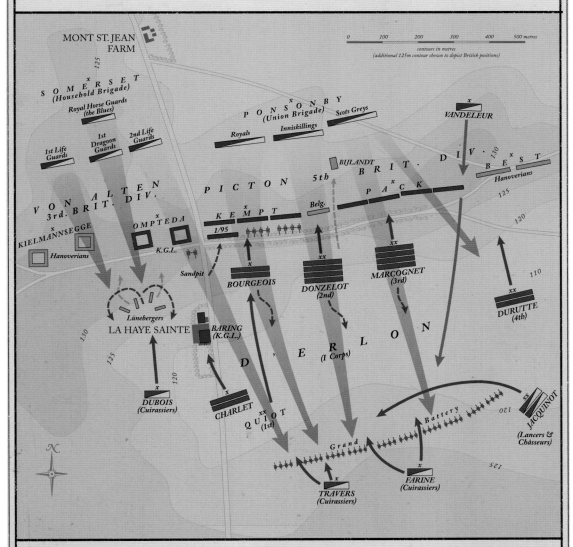

D'ERLON'S INFANTRY ATTACK AND UXBRIDGE'S CALVARY COUNTER ATTACK
2PM, 18 JUNE 1815

MONT ST. JEAN FARM

0   100   200   300   400   500 metres
contours in metres
(additional 125m contour shown to depict British positions)

S O M E R S E T
(Household Brigade)

Royal Horse Guards
(the Blues)

P O N S O N B Y
(Union Brigade)   Scots Greys

VANDELEUR

1st
Dragoon
Guards

2nd Life
Guards

Royals   Inniskillings

1st Life
Guards

BIJLANDT   BRIT.   DIV.   B E S T

Hanoverians

V O N   A L T E N   P I C T O N   5th   P A C K

3rd. BRIT. DIV.   Belg.

KIELMANNSEGGE   O M P T E D A   K E M P T

Hanoverians   K.G.L.   1/95

Sandpit   BOURGEOIS   DONZELOT   MARCOGNET
                                                        (2nd)   (3rd)

Lüneburgers   DURUTTE
LA HAYE SAINTE   BARING
(K.G.L.)   D ' E R L O N   (4th)

DUBOIS   (I Corps)
(Cuirassiers)   CHARLET
                              Q U I O T   Battery   JACQUINOT
                              (1st)
                                                                  (Lancers &
                                                                  Chasseurs)
                    Grand

                              TRAVERS   FARINE
                              (Cuirassiers)   (Cuirassiers)

NAPOLEON'S GRAND BATTERY OF GUNS bombards Wellington's line from late morning.

D'Erlon launches his massed attack on Wellington's left at 2pm. The Dutch-Belgians and the 1/95th Rifles retreat behind the ridge. Baring's battalion of the King's German Legion hold onto La Haye Sainte but are almost completely surrounded. The French scatter a force of Luneburgers attempting to support Baring.

The British heavy cavalry – the Household and Union brigades – attack and destroy d'Erlon's infantry assault but they then charge in among the French guns and are hit from both sides by fresh French cavalry.

Vandeleur's light cavalry brigade attempts to come to the rescue. It too is hard hit.

close columns in the Peninsular War made d'Erlon stretch his battalions out in lines up to 150 men wide and three ranks deep. The more muskets with unobstructed fire, the better. It must have taken at least 20 minutes for these vast unwieldy formations – drums playing, banners flying – to squelch their way up through the rye that rose nearly 2 metres (6 feet) from the muddy ground. They were under allied gunfire all the way, but they made quick gains. A Dutch-Belgian brigade that Wellington had placed in their path on the forward slope quickly retreated behind the ridge. The defenders of La Haye Sainte were forced back out of the garden and orchard into the walled precinct. Even the nearby outpost of the riflemen of the elite 95th – who had made good use of their longer range weapons by picking off as many of the advancing Frenchmen as they could – had to pull back.

As the first French ranks reached the

Above: A carbine, a shortened, more wieldy musket designed for use by dragoons, cavalrymen who were expected to fire from their saddles or dismount and fight on foot.

Left: The eagle battle standard of the French 105th Infantry Regiment captured by Captain Alexander Kennedy Clark of the 1st Royal Dragoons. Capturing an imperial eagle was the highest achievement imaginable, and Clark's claim to have taken it was disputed by another member of his regiment.

Opposite, top: There is a degree of fantasy in this image of Highlanders heroically taking on French *cuirassiers*. In the reality, infantry stood little chance of defending themselves against cavalry attacks unless they bunched together in squares.

Left: The death of Lieutenant-General Sir Thomas Picton. Picton's luggage had not arrived so he fought in his civilian coat and top hat. Many key personnel on both sides were killed or injured, and it is remarkable that Wellington, on the allied side, and Ney, on the French, were unscathed: both were consistently in the thick of the fighting.

top of the ridge and crossed the sunken road, the British and their allies rose to confront them. Wellington's left centre was manned by around 3,500 British infantry – all Peninsular veterans – under the redoubtable Picton and two neighbouring Hanoverian brigades. The odds were heavily stacked against them but they were defenders, fresh and eager for action against attackers battered by artillery and somewhat breathless after their climb. Picton's men were just behind the brow of the hill, and as their enemy burst into view they fired a volley and heard their general shout, "Charge! Charge! Hurrah! Hurrah!" These were Picton's last words – seconds later he was lying dead, a musket ball in his brain.

The huge melee that followed as the two sides clashed on the ridge was a frantic struggle, and both sides knew its outcome could open the road to Brussels for Napoleon. The allies fired volley after volley, and charged the attackers with bayonets. Some French units were halted while others turned in retreat, but more kept coming on.

Wellington's line was thinly spread. He had few ready reserves to throw in to reinforce any gaps and it was the first of many critical moments for the duke's army. In the end, it was his cavalry who came to the rescue.

Wellington had serious doubts about his cavalry. His horsemen had let him down in the Peninsular War by – as he described it – "galloping at everything" without much thought. Besides, his cavalry commander, Lord Uxbridge – who had many years earlier run off with Wellington's sister-in-law – was not the man he would have chosen. Uxbridge had been imposed on him by the Duke of York, his overall commander-in-chief in London. But Uxbridge was now to prove his worth with a brilliant though ultimately very costly master-stroke. He ordered his entire force of more than 2,000 British heavy cavalrymen to charge d'Erlon's now struggling French infantry.

There were seven heavy cavalry regiments – three in the Union Brigade (the First – or Royal – Dragoons recruited in England, the Irish Inniskillings and the Scots Greys), and

four in the Household Brigade (the First and Second Life Guards, the Royal Horse Guards and the King's Dragoon Guards). They were magnificently mounted on horses superior to those of their French rivals, whose supply of strong steeds had been weakened by two decades of Continental warfare. But the British were less experienced at fighting and French cavalry sabres were 15 cm (6 inches) longer.

At Uxbridge's command, the bugles sounded. He took the lead himself with Lord Edward Somerset's Household Brigade on the left and Major-General Sir William Ponsonby's Union Brigade on the right. They moved forward and, pausing at the sunken road to form two extended lines, careered into the throng. The Household Brigade smashed its way through a large force of *cuirassiers* around La Haye Sainte and into the left flank of d'Erlon's infantry. They

carried all before them, slashing and stabbing their way through opponents bewildered by the suddenness of the British charge.

The Union Brigade tackled d'Erlon's infantry assault head on. As the Scots Greys swept past the British defenders on the ridge, some Gordon Highlanders shouted, "Scotland for ever". What followed was carnage on a horrific scale. As the French infantry turned and fled, flashing sabres cut off arms, legs and heads. Some escaped by feigning death, lying down as the cavalry pounded over them. Two thousand surrendered. D'Erlon's great attack was shredded.

However, the British cavalry's triumph was short-lived. Buoyed up by their success, their bravery became recklessly suicidal. "On to the guns," shouted some, spotting the artillery of the *Grande Batterie* up the slope ahead. "On to Paris," shouted others. All discipline collapsed: Uxbridge later said how much he regretted being at the head of the charge when by staying back a little he might have exerted some control. Some of his men reached the guns while others galloped around attacking in all directions. Within minutes, their horses were breathless and their momentum spent. They were at the mercy of a number of French cavalry counter-attacks. *Cuirassiers* and lancers, whose long weapons far outreached the cavalry's sabres, surrounded the men of the two brigades who had now been broken up into small groups. Hundreds died or were severely wounded. Ponsonby, who had swapped his charger for a much weaker horse that morning, was isolated and cut down. And when a brigade of British light cavalry charged in to restore the balance, another Ponsonby – Sir William's cousin Lieutenant-Colonel Frederick – was wounded by a lancer when he too led his men too far.

The British cavalry had been virtually destroyed. Some regiments lost around half their strength. Wellington knew there would be little they could do for the rest of the battle. He was heard to remark to Uxbridge, addressing him by his ordinary family name, "Well, Paget, I hope you are satisfied with your cavalry now."

However, Uxbridge's charge had destroyed Napoleon's first great onslaught and time was turning inexorably against the French. The Prussians were now beginning to attack and Napoleon knew there was no hope of Grouchy rejoining him before the following day. The emperor summoned Marshal Ney and urgently told him to use every resource he could to punch his way through Wellington's line.

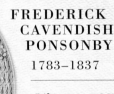

FREDERICK CAVENDISH PONSONBY

1783–1837

Like many of Wellington's officers, Ponsonby was an aristocrat. He was the second son of the 3rd Earl of Bessborough and the brother of Lord Byron's lover Lady Caroline Lamb. A superb horseman, he commanded the 12th Light Dragoons in the Peninsular War and at Waterloo. After he had been lanced on the battlefield, he lay in agony all night, narrowly avoiding being crushed by galloping cavalry. A kind Frenchman took pity on him and gave him a swig of brandy. Ponsonby recovered from his wounds and later became a general and Governor of Malta. He was surprised and delighted when years later his benefactor turned up in a French military delegation to the island.

Instructions for the cavalry issued by Colonel Sir John Elley, Deputy Adjutant-General and written into the Order Book of the 7th Hussars. Before the Battle of Waterloo, the orders include postal arrangements, the composition of recruiting parties, the requisitioning of flints for carbines, and an urgent injunction that the heavy cavalry's swords be ground to a point, so that they can be used for thrusting as well as cutting. After the Battle, casualty returns needs to be compiled, absent officers recalled to their regiments, stragglers rounded up, and patrols operating in advance of the army reminded to report on the state of the roads. The later orders are issued by Major Michael Childers after Elley was wounded:

G.C.O.   Ninove 12th June 1815
Nº.1
The swords of every Regiment of Cavalry are to be ground & pointed, according to the pattern received by the Troop Sgt. Majors and men assembled this Day at Cavalry Head Quarters.

2. The order must be carried into execution without Loss of Time.
Signed
J Elly Col
DAG

G.C.O.   Ninove 13th June 1815
1. The Commander of the Forces having made known to the Earl of Uxbridge his Intention to send recruiting Parties to Hanover. The Field Officers, Captains, Lieutenants, Cornets, Sergeants and Corporals as undermentioned will assemble at Antwerp without delay for the Purpose of proceeding on this Duty.

2.   Detail

	F.O.	–	Capt	–	Lieut	–	xxx	–	Sgts	–	Corpls
1st – Dragoons	•	—	1	—	•	—	•	—	1	—	4
2nd Dº [ditto]	•	—	•	—	1	—	1	—	1	—	4
1st Hussars	1	—	•	—	1	—	•	—	1	—	4
2nd Dº	•	—	•	—	1	—	1	—	1	—	4
3rd Dº	•	—	1	—	•	—	1	—	1	—	4
Total	1	—	2	—	3	—	3	—	5	—	20

3. Major Muller 1st Hussars and Captn Hoyers of the 3rd Hussars are to be the Field Officer and Captain furnish'd by those Regts according to the above Detail.
4. The whole to be under the Charge of Major Muller to whom each Detacht will report on its arrival at Antwerp.
5. The Sgts and Corpls are to be dismounted and their Horses left with their respective Regiments.
Signed
J Elly, Col
DAG

G.C.O.   Therres 19th June 1815
In pursuance of Directions from the Commr of the Forces, two Offrs of each Reg. of Cavalry will be sent immediately to the Rear for the Purpose of collecting the Stragglers of their respective Corps.
The Commr of the Forces also requests that the practices of firing their Carbines in Camp may be discontinued, when it is necessary the Men must be assembled under an Offr.
In compliance with G. Orders the following Letter parties will parade at ½ past 8 O'Clock this Evening at Coll Sleigh's Quarters and proceed to Nivelle & there report themselves to the Adjt Genl.

	Corpls	Privts
11th		2
12 — Dº	1	2
16 — Dº		2
Total	1	6

G.C.O.   23rd June 1815
Nº.1 Returns of casualties to be sent this Afternoon according to the Accompg Form, accounting for each Day separately, the Return will be sent in Duplicates, the Christian Names of the Offrs to be inserted at length.
2. States of the Cavalry both Weekly and Daily will be sent in as soon as possible from the 14th Inst, Returns of the Casualties of the Genl Staff will be sent in this Day from the Brigades to which they were attached.

G.C.O.   Croix, June 25th 1815
Nº.1 Segt Mattw Billingay 11th Lt Dns is appointed to act as an Asst Baggage Master until further Orders[.] He will proceed Mounted to Hd Qrs this Day and report himself to the A.A.Adjt Genl.
2. Genls and Offrs in Comd of Brigades are requested to the G.O. dated 30 Apr 1815. No 2 & G.C.O. dated 10th May 1815 Nº 1 & are requested to order in immediately all Dragoons that may be absent except those furnished by Genl or G.C. Orders.
Sd M Childers
Majr A A Adjt Gl

G.C.O.   Esheliers 26th June 1815
Nº.1 Officers on outpost Duty will be pleased to make regular Reports to Cavalry Hd Qrs daily of the Information obtained by their Patroles of the State of Roads and Features of the Country in front.

35

G.C.O)   Ninove 12.th June 1815

No 1   The Swords of every Regiment of
Cavalry are to be ground & painted.
according to the Pattern recieved by
the Troop Serj.t Majors and Men
assembled this Day at Cavalry Head
Quarters: —

2   This Order must be carried into
execution without Loss of Time. —

            Signed

                J Elley Col.t
                 D.A.G —

G.C.O)   Ninove, 13.th June 1815

1   The Comm.t of the Forces having made known
to the Earl of Uxbridge, his intention to send
recruiting Parties to Hanover. The Field
Officers, Captains, Lieutenants, Cornets
Serjeants and Corporals as undermentioned
will assemble at Antwerp without Delay

for the Purpose of proceeding on this Duty

Detail

2

	F.O.	Capt	Liut	Corn	S.s	Corp.	
1.st L. Dragoons	"	—	1	—	,	—	"	—	1	—	4
2.o Do	"	—	"	—	,	—	"	—	1	—	4
1.st Kussars	1	—	"	—	1	—	1	—	1	—	4
2.o Do	"	—	1	—	"	—	"	—	1	—	4
3.o Do	"	—	"	—	1	—	1	—	1	—	4
	"	—	"	—	1	—	"	—	1	—	4
Total	1	— 2	— 3	— 3	— 5	— 20

3 Majr Muller 1st Kussars & Captn Kayer
of the 3.d Kussars are to be the Field Off.
and Captain furnish'd by those Regts
acording to the above Detail. —

4 The whole to be under the Charge of
Major Muller to whom each Detacht
will report on its arrival at Antwerp

5 The Supr Horsr are to be dismounted
and their Horses left with their respective
Regiments. —

Signed J. Eley Col.

A.G.

G. C. O)   Therres, 19th June 1815.

In pursuance of Directions from the Commr of the Forces, two Offrs of each Regt of Cavalry will be sent immediately to the Rear for the Purpose of collecting the Stragglers of their respective Corps.

The Commr of the Forces also requests that the Practice of firing their Carbines in Camp may be discontinued, when it is necessary the Men must be assembled under an Offr.

In compliance with G. Orders the following Letter parties will parade at ½ past 6 O'Clock this Evening at Coll Sleighs Quarters and proceed to Nouville there report themselves to the Adjt Genl

	Corpls	Privts
11th Lt Dns		2
12 do	1	2
16 do		2
Total	1	6

No 1   Returns of Casualtys to be sent this
Afternoon according to the accomp⁹
Form, accounting for each Day
separately, this Return will be sent
in Duplicate, the Christian Names
of the Offⁿˢ to be inserted at length

2   States of the Cavalry both Weekly
and Daily will be sent in as soon
as possible from the 14ᵗʰ Inˢᵗ; Returns
of the Casualties of the Gen.ˡ Staff
will be sent in this Day from the
Brigades to which they were attach⁴

G. C. O)   Croix, June 25ᵗʰ —

No 1   Serj.ᵗ Matt.ʰᵉʷ Billingay 11ᵗʰ L.ᵗ D.ⁿˢ
is appointed to act as an Ass.ᵗ Baj⁰
Master untill further Orders he
will proceed Mounted to H.ᵈ Q⁰ˢ

this Day and report himself to the
A. A. Adjt. Genl.

2 — Genl. and Offr. in Comd. of Brigades
are referred to the G.O. dated 30 Apr.
1815. No. 2 & G.C.O. dated 10th May 1815
No. 1 and 11th June 1815 No. 1 & are requested
to order in immediately all Dragoons
that may be absent except those
furnished by Genl. or G.C. Orders —

            Sd. M. Childers
            Majr. A. A. Adjt. Gl.

G.C.O }   Eshelers, 26th June 1815

No. 1   ——— Officers on outpost Duty will
be pleased to make regular Reports
to Cavalry H. Qrs. daily of the information
obtained by their Patroles & the State
of Roads and Features of the Country
in front. ———

PRIVATE SAMUEL BOULTER

25 SEPTEMBER 1815

Private Samuel Boulter of the 2nd Dragoons (or Scots Greys) writes to his brother from Rouen on 25 September 1815 with his account of the battle. In this extract he describes his horror on viewing the carnage wrought by the battle:

"… [Those of the French] that Did get away run as if the Devil had been hard after them, threw off their Nabsacks and left every thing they was possessed off and can assure you no small number was lying on the Ground next Day[.] But it was a very affecting scene to see so many men lying Dead in such a short time for my part I cannot ascribe it to any thing else than a Judgement of God and indeed a great many lay Wounded which called for Water but we could not supply them all some were lying with legs off some Wounded all over the Body in such a manner that they were not able to move a yard[.] We buried all of ours that was Dead that we could find and the Wounded was taken off and Medical assistance was rendered them immediately[.] I can assure you some of the poor fellows was most terribly cut up several has Died since of their Wounds and almost every one that had a limb amputated has Died. However I have reason to thank that Superintending providence that [h]as hitherto guarded me from all Dangers and hope that matters will take such a turn as will soon restore all people to their homes …"

off and Medical apistance we rendered them imm-
mediate, I can assure you some of the poor fellows are
most truilly cut up several has died since of there
Wounds and almost every one that had a limb amputed
has died, However I have reason to thank that superintending providence that as hitherto guarded me from
all Dangers and hope that Matters will take such a
turn as will soon restore all people to their homes
However We continued our march and got up within
5 Mile Off Paris and remained there some time
When We marched to this place and can assure
you we had a very pretty March the weather was
good and almost every thing was in bloom the
people had Apple trees all the Way on the road
side and indeed the Crops in General was very
good but their Farmes are not able to come up
with ours for a great many things for here so many
Different ways of contriving things and so Dirty constructs
that it is impossible to give you any Idea of it
The people are very poor in this county the laser
clep of people chiefly live on bread — their potatoes
are very good but there bread they Make is so
bitter that in the course of a short time its gets moldy
I cannot give you any more particulars at present
but & in my next I shall give you more

You Dont mention any thing about my
sister Mary whether she is living or not should be glad to
hear how you all are and write soon as you can
make it convenient and give my love to Mother &
Sisters & all Friend and relations and accept the
same Yourself and am Dear William Your
ever affectionate Brother
Samuel Boulter

P. S. I cannot conclude without begging you
will present my love to your Mrs & Children and hope
they are all Well Write soon and let me know
how sister Mary is

them latters
~ about 48
...up We was
...assure you
...from until
...y has not
...ishes in reading
remain cont
...jects begin to
...t 12 Black
...Colleums
Men and
Prisoners and
...rincipals Eagle
the times.—
...d we continued
...age we had
...came of the
...uch by that time
...nerals Personly
...immense stores
...which her
...soon after
Ranks and
...dy, But
...up an
not experd
while our
Down 20 &
...r un as he
...all their
...apposed off
...being on the
...ry affecting
...D in they such
...souls it to
...and indeed
...tter for Water
...some wer
...l over the
...and able to
...t was Dead
...were taker

THE GREAT FRENCH CALVARY ATTACKS

NOBODY KNOWS FOR SURE whether it was Napoleon himself who gave the order for what followed next. He later claimed that it was Marshal Ney who took it upon himself to send the great mass of French cavalry into a prodigious set of attacks on the allied ridge. Those who witnessed it claimed that it was the most astonishing spectacle they had ever seen. The bloodshed on both sides was on a dreadful scale.

It was around 4pm when Ney spotted what he thought was the beginnings of an enemy retreat. He was mistaken, but he used the opportunity to re-establish his reputation as Napoleon's most fiery and audacious commander. Placing himself at the head of the cavalry corps, Ney was to have several horses shot dead under him as he led a series of cavalry charges by more than 8,000 horsemen that lasted for two hours. With a cry of "Forward! The salvation of France is at stake," Ney led the first wave forward.

Those of Wellington's men who could see beyond the top of the ridge that sheltered them spotted what "glittered like a stormy wave of the sea when it catches the sunlight". It was a long line of horsemen advancing towards them. As the French cavalry approached, the ground trembled

Below: Marshal Michel Ney (on the white horse) leads one of the many French cavalry charges at Waterloo. He had five horses shot under him in the course of the battle.

FRENCH CAVALRY ATTACKS AND THE PRUSSIAN ADVANCE
4–6PM, 18 JUNE 1815

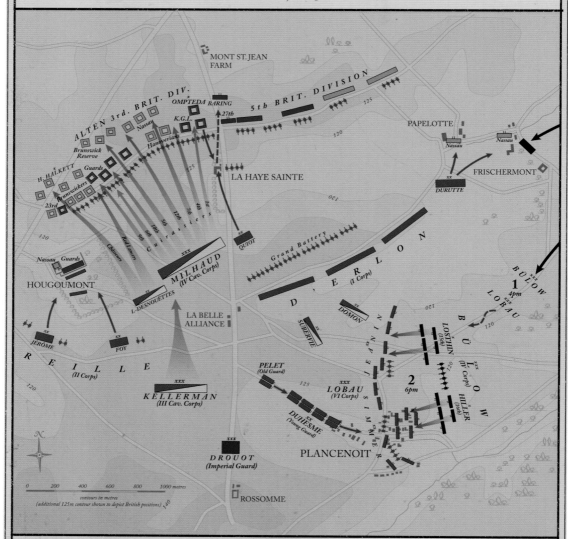

MONT ST. JEAN FARM

ALTEN 3rd. BRIT. DIV.

OMPTEDA BARING

5 t h B R I T. D I V I S I O N

27th

Nassau

K.G.L.

Brunswick
Reserve

Hanoverian

125

PAPELOTTE

120

H. HALKETT   Guards

Brunswickers

23rd

Nassau

Nassau

LA HAYE SAINTE

FRISCHERMONT

120

1st
7th   4th
12th
5th
10th
9th   Cuirassiers

xx
DURUTTE

Chasseurs

Red Lancers

QUIOT

125

xxx
MILHAUD
(IV Cav. Corps)

Nassau   Guards

Grand Battery

130

D '   E R L O N
(I Corps)

120

B Ü L O W

1
4pm

HOUGOUMONT

L-DESNOUETTES

D.

J E N N I N

DOMON

xx

B
Ü
L
O
W
(IV Corps)

xxx

LOSTHIN
(15th)

120

LA BELLE
ALLIANCE

xx
JEROME

xx
FOY

SUBERVIE

xx

120

2
6pm

R   E   I   L   L   E
(II Corps)

120

PELET
(Old Guard)

125

xxx
LOBAU
(VI Corps)

T H Ü M E N

HILLER
(16th)

xxx
KELLERMAN
(III Cav. Corps)

DUHESME
(Young Guard)

xxx
DROUOT
(Imperial Guard)

PLANCENOIT

0   200   400   600   800   1000 metres

contours in metres
(additional 125m contour shown to depict British positions)   140

ROSSOMME

A T AROUND 4PM, MARSHAL NEY LEADS Milhaud's corps of heavy cavalry and Lefebvre-Desnouettes' Imperial Guard cavalry against Wellington's right. Kellerman's cavalry corps continues the offensive from 5pm. British and allied battalions form squares, and resist wave after wave of attacks for two hours.

At 6pm Baring's men at La Haye Sainte run out of ammunition and the French capture the farm. Another KGL battalion under Colonel Ompteda attempting to reach the farm is overwhelmed and the Colonel killed. The French move guns up to La Haye

Sainte and their fire almost destroys the 27th regiment of foot – the Inniskillings – in the centre of Wellington's front line

The Prussians attack Napoleon's right at 4pm. Napoleon diverts Lobau's corps to protect his flank but (1) they fail to hold back Bülow's Prussians. By 6pm (2) the battle with the Prussians has shifted to the village of Plancenoit. Lobau is under such pressure that Napoleon sends the Young Guard and two battalions of the Old Guard to reinforce him. For a time the French succeed in holding the village.

at the pounding of hooves. The bright colours and flashing helmets of General Milhaud's cavalry corps could soon be made out. Most frightening of all, though, was the sight of the breast-plated cuirassiers, each one of them at least 1.8 metres (6 feet) tall and mounted on the heaviest horses. Behind them trotted the 1,200 men of the *Chasseurs à Cheval*, elite light cavalry from the Emperor's Imperial Guard decked out in green and gold.

Wellington's men had been expecting an attack because after d'Erlon's defeat French guns opened up on the units on the allied right. Nearly all the men were behind the ridge, so few of the cannonballs landed among them. But then Wellington's order sounded across the whole front: "Prepare to receive cavalry!" Within minutes, the whole of the duke's force had reshuffled from lines into some 30 squares – one for each battalion. The sides of each square were four ranks deep, men facing out with bayonets fixed. Horses always stopped short of impaling themselves on the bayonets of men who stuck to that rigid formation. However, any gap in the square and the cavalry would be in and slashing the battalion to pieces.

Some but not all of Wellington's exposed artillery out in front of the squares held their ground as the French cavalry closed with them. Those that stood – including the resourceful Captain Mercer and his troop

of horse artillerymen – rapidly loaded their guns with case shot. When blown out of the barrel, each canister hurled 44 three-ounce balls in an expanding circle that hit the assaulting cavalry at a range of about 50 metres (164 feet). The resulting destruction was devastating: horses and riders crashed to the ground causing a bloody pile-up of dead and wounded men and animals that for a moment blunted the attack. The gunners who hadn't time to run back into the nearest square ducked for cover under their guns as the charge recovered its momentum and swept on against the squares.

It is not difficult to imagine the terror that must have seized the infantrymen facing a charging cuirassier. The temptation to turn and run must have been overwhelming, particularly for the thousands of new recruits who had never seen anything like this before. Some of the men had been at Quatre Bras and had seen how the squares that held fast survived. But many were in it for the first time. Officers inside the squares shouted encouragement and the occasional threat if a rank showed signs of weakness. And then the cuirassiers and the other cavalrymen were upon them. Some were shot down or had their horse killed under them as they came close. Others raced around the squares crying *"Vive L'Empereur"* and watching for a gap to appear before charging ahead to the next line of squares.

Above: The Duke of Wellington shouts encouragement to an infantry square at Waterloo. He is carrying his trademark telescope, to keep an anxious eye on his advancing Prussian allies. The British redcoats, in square with bayonets at the ready, have just fought off a charge by French *cuirassiers* – one lies dead in the foreground. On the left British gunners struggle to reload in the face of a new cavalry charge.

Below: Cuirassiers charging a Scottish square. A white horse appears (perhaps an exaggeration by the artist) to be impaled on the bayonets of the Highlanders. Horses usually recoil from the blades as long as the infantrymen maintain their formation. Many more horses lie dead or dying from gunshot wounds.

Wellington was everywhere as the pressure of the French cavalry charges intensified. He was in and out of the squares, shouting encouragement and urging the men to close any gaps. Many of Wellington's aides were killed or wounded. Although the duke was often under fire, miraculously he remained unscathed. His first impression was that the squares were holding and the French horsemen, circling and frantically trying to break through, were being held off. Some noticed him looking at his watch and he was heard to say, "The battle is mine and if the Prussians arrive soon, there will be an end of the war."

However, as the French first wave withdrew utterly exhausted, the artillery bombardment opened up again. And once the horses had recovered, Ney's cavalry returned again and again to attack the increasingly battered allied squares. Within another hour, allied officers on the brow of the hill with telescopes could see that an entire second corps of cavalry, up to 3,500 horsemen under General Kellerman, were moving up to reinforce Milhaud's corps. Kellerman brought with him squadrons of lancers with 2.7-metre- (9-foot-) long blades that they could thrust past the defenders' bayonets or hurl at the sides of the squares as they swept past.

Allied infantryman Tom Morris – a Londoner and still a teenager – described how he was kneeling in the front rank when a *cuirassier* approached and thrust his long sword at him. "I saw it coming and involuntarily closed my eyes." However, when he looked again, his antagonist "was falling to the ground with his horse… killed, and the rider wounded by some efficient shots from my rear." Morris watched with horrified admiration as the wounded *cuirassier* then unsuccessfully tried to kill himself with his sword; the man then held himself up with one hand, placed a bayonet into a gap in his cuirass and fell on it.

The bravery and tenacity of the French cavalrymen, as they charged again and again,

Left, top: A French dragoon's helmet, believed to have been picked up on the field of Waterloo. French dragoons - unlike the British - still dismounted on occasion to act as foot soldiers.

Left, Below: A French *cuirassier's* breast plate found by a British doctor after the battle. Although it withstood sabre cuts, musket and rifle balls could penetrate it.

won grudging admiration from many who survived their attacks. The corpses of men and horses lay scattered around the squares, and the groans and screams of the wounded mixed with the roar of cannon and the crack of muskets. But the men in the squares were suffering too. One infantryman remembered not being able to move without treading upon a dead or wounded comrade: "Our square was a perfect hospital, being full of dead, dying and wounded soldiers." Mercer lost 140 out of 200 horses, and a third of his men. Some commanders were close to despair and one appealed to Wellington:

"Can you not relieve us for a little while?"

"Impossible," came the reply, "I must have British troops in front".

"Enough my lord, we'll stand here till the last man falls."

Somehow, over the two-hour duration of these attacks, the squares held. Uxbridge did his best to relieve the pressure by ordering his remaining cavalry in to chase the French each time they retreated. They were unable to make much difference. One allied unit, the Cumberland Hussars, found it all too much and left the field for Brussels. Panic ensued as many people assumed the allies had been beaten.

However, each French charge became a little less fierce than the one before. Kellerman was wounded and Milhaud was unhorsed. At 6pm, Ney called off what had become a futile offensive. The British line was still intact and the great cavalry action had failed. Napoleon had felt unable to give close support to the cavalry with infantry and artillery. One French cavalry officer wrote of how the absence of infantry and artillery to support the attack had determined the retreat: "We were hoping the Emperor's genius would change the face of battle, by organising an all arms attack… but nothing! Absolutely nothing!"

The French charges had been funnelled through the gap between La Haye Sainte and Hougoumont, making them vulnerable to allied fire from their flanks. It had been a glorious but costly failure. No certain count has ever been made of the number of French casualties; however, from that point, Napoleon's cavalry was a spent force.

The Emperor now faced what appeared to be unshakeable resistance on the ridge ahead of him and what had since developed into a full battle with the Prussians on his right. Another commander-in-chief might have decided that the time had come for a strategic withdrawal; Napoleon, however, determined to fight on.

Above: A light cavalry officer's sword believed to have been carried in the battle by Lieutenant Henry Lane of the 15th Hussars. The grip inside the stirrup-shaped guard is made of leather. In his account of the battle, Lane later reported: "During the day we were constantly on the move, attacking and retreating to our lines." By the end of the battle, he says, "We were dreadfully cut up."

FRANÇOIS ÉTIENNE DE KELLERMAN
1770–1835

Small and sickly, Kellerman, 2nd Duc de Valmy, was known as "the ugliest man in the army". Under the patronage of his famous father, Marshal François Christophe de Kellerman, he became an outstanding cavalry commander. One of Napoleon's longest-serving soldiers, Kellerman fought the British under Wellington in Portugal and Spain. His reputation was sullied by widespread plundering when he was Acting Commander of the army in Castile. Kellerman later boasted, "I did not cross the Alps merely for my health." His daring charges at Quatre Bras captured a colour of the British 69th Foot and forced other Allied units to flee. When his horse was killed, Kellerman escaped by hanging on to the stirrups of fellow troopers' horses.

Though I cannot persuade myself that
the wish that you once so kindly expressed
is stile as lively as then, yet not to see
you as you appear to see me, I write
to say that I suffered no harm from the Affair
of yesterday. even although the chance has not
How brilliant & decisive it arrived.
was, the Gazette will inform you; I only send
these few lines written according to your desire
in hurry & confusion to assure you that
in spite of your forgetfulness, my affection

PRIVATE PHILIP WODEHOUSE
19 AUGUST 1815

Private Philip Wodehouse of the 15th Hussars writes the day after Waterloo to his faithless love, Miss Parry:

> *"Though I cannot persuade myself that the wish that you once so kindly expressed is still as lively as then, yet not to use you as you appear to use me, I write to say that I suffered no harm from the affair of yesterday even although the charm has not arrived. How brilliant & decisive it was, the Gazette will inform you; I only send you these few lines written according to your desire in hurry & confusion to assure you that in spite of your forgetfulness, my affection for you is as strong as ever, & that if a cannon ball hits me tomorrow I believe I shall die thinking of you."*

THE ARRIVAL
OF THE
PRUSSIANS

WELLINGTON WAS WELL SERVED by his Prussian ally Field Marshal Gebhard von Blücher. The Prussian commander had promised Wellington, whom he referred to as his "brother", that he would arrive with two corps – up to 50,000 men – in time to support him in the battle that day. If any of the Prussian generals had been dubious about the wisdom of going to the duke's aid, Blücher soon disabused them. Once he had shaken off the effects of his fall at Ligny, and refreshed himself with a good draught or two of Prussian beer, he exerted his authority and insisted that three of his corps should march westwards and join battle with Wellington against Napoleon. "Ill and old as I am, I will nevertheless ride at the head of my men to attack the enemy's right wing at once, should Napoleon make any move against the duke."

Wellington spent much of the day anxiously training his telescope on the woods way over to his left hoping to see the Prussians emerge into the open. Blücher's problem was the appalling condition of the track that led from Wavre to Waterloo. It took his leading units, those of Count von Bülow (the commander of the Prussian IV Corps), some 12 hours to pass through Wavre and cover the 24 km (15 miles) to Waterloo. The first scouts and skirmishers had appeared from the wood and alerted Napoleon hours earlier, but the main

body of the Prussian force was well behind. Blücher, exasperated at the delay, rode up and down among his men passionately urging them to get a move on: "Come on boys, don't say it can't be done. I promised my brother Wellington. Do you want to make me a liar?"

It wasn't until after Marshal Ney had led two or three of his massed cavalry charges against Wellington's line that the Prussians began to emerge in some strength. By 4.30pm, columns of black uniformed Prussians were becoming visible. Wellington sent a message to them asking them to reinforce his own left wing so that he could move men to plug the weak points in his centre. But Bülow decided that rather than join up with the allies directly, he would take the battle to Napoleon. The Prussians were burning to get at the French, to avenge their defeat at Ligny and the suffering and indignity that Napoleon had inflicted on Prussia over his years of rule. They headed straight for Napoleon's vulnerable flank, the village of Plancenoit.

Bülow immediately threw his troops into battle with the French in and around the village. He had the advantage of numbers: his 30,000 men outnumbered his French opponents by as much as 3 to 1. But Bülow's men were tired, hungry and exhausted after a long march and little sleep the night before. Besides, two thirds of his men were Landwehr, recently recruited trainees. The experienced French commander Lobau, on the other hand, was defending the village with fresh troops. The fight was long and fierce, but all the time Bülow's strength was being reinforced by more of his men pressing forward through the woods. By 6.30pm, Lobau had been pushed back to the centre of the village. Blücher sent in further reinforcements as his other corps moved towards the battlefield. General Ziethen moved in to bolster Wellington's line and allow him to shift some forces to where he was weakest. Meanwhile, General Pirch moved his corps up behind Bülow's to give him direct support.

The odds against the French in Plancenoit were now overwhelming. Napoleon was earnestly contemplating his next move after Ney's cavalry attacks had battered Wellington's right but failed to break through. The battle against Wellington's centre was now in full swing but Napoleon knew that the loss of Plancenoit would be a crippling reverse: the village must be held. He felt that he had no choice but to reinforce the men who had been fighting valiantly but under increasing pressure for the past two hours. If he didn't take urgent action, he risked catastrophic defeat – and time was running out. There was little more than two or three hours of daylight left: Napoleon had

to defeat Wellington before dark or he would be at the mercy of the entire combined allied and Prussian armies the following day.

There can be no doubt that the impact of Blücher's attack was already deeply damaging Napoleon's effort to smash through Wellington's line. Lobau's entire corps, some 10,000 men, had been intended as a reserve to throw against Wellington when the time was right. It was now totally engaged against the Prussians. And so, with Lobau desperate for reinforcement, Napoleon felt he had to dig further into his reserves. Reluctantly he sent an order to General Duhesme, commander of the Young Guard, to lead his eight battalions – nearly 5,000 men – to rescue Lobau. Yet more of Napoleon's precious reserve was now being committed against Blücher. The Young Guard, the frontline troops of the Imperial Guard and usually the first ones to engage, was the least privileged and least experienced of the emperor's elite forces. But these troops were highly respected: everyone knew that Duhesme's men were trained and motivated by the grizzled veterans of the Imperial Guard.

It was around 6.30pm. The Young Guard, fresh into the fray, soon dislodged Bülow's men from the centre of Plancenoit, and within minutes had them retreating fast out of the village. The diversion of this vital

Below: Marshal Emmanuel de Grouchy on the march to Wavre in pursuit of the Prussians (wood engraving). Some of his commanders are urging him to change direction and head towards the sound of the guns from Waterloo. He ignored their advice and failed to go to Napoleon's rescue.

reserve postponed for a time the crisis on Napoleon's right. It left him fewer troops to pursue his plans in the centre (see below), but he hoped that Duhesme's men would be sufficient to rebuff Blücher. Napoleon now resorted to one reckless piece of deceit to put heart into his men on other fronts. He sent his aides racing to tell all his other units that the sounds they could hear over their right shoulders were those of Grouchy's men rejoining the contest. *"Soldats! Voila Grouchy. Vive L'Empereur!"*

Napoleon himself had now lost all hope of seeing Grouchy on the field that day,

but he must have reckoned this desperate stratagem might just boost morale as the battle approached its final stages. It may have worked for some. But for others, the Prussian presence was all too real – Prussian shells were already arriving in the French centre where the Imperial Guard waited in reserve. There were also reports circulating that the emperor's personal staff were packing his bags in readiness for a quick move. "From then on," recalled one Imperial Guard officer, "no one thought any longer of going to Brussels."

The battle for Plancenoit was as fierce as any on the field of Waterloo. It was fought

Above: Prussians at the town of Wavre fight off attacks to their rearguard by Marshal Grouchy. They had been defeated and forced to retreat from Ligny on 16 June. In spite of Grouchy's efforts, Marshal Blücher was able to dispatch three of his corps with all speed to attack Napoleon's right wing at Waterloo. Many of them managed to reach the battlefield and help their allies to victory.

Overleaf: The Battle of Plancenoit, late afternoon 18 June. Fighting at close quarters raged within the village for several hours. The increasing pressure of the Prussians on his right flank forced Napoleon to divert some of his best men from the Old Guard (on the left here) - troops sorely needed to confront Wellington.

house by house, sometimes at very close quarters. The French Young Guard and what were left of Lobau's men fought with great courage. Bülow himself acknowledged that "the village of Plancenoit was stubbornly defended by the elite of the enemy".

However, once again the steadily growing weight of the Prussians began to tell. Pirch's men were now moving in to support Bülow. By 7pm, the French defenders were in desperate straits. The Young Guard's commander, General Duhesme, had been fatally wounded.

Napoleon had seen enough to regret bitterly that he had only damaged rather than destroyed the Prussian army at Ligny. Blücher's men were showing startling resilience only three days after their defeat, and Napoleon had no choice but to slice even further into his precious reserve. This time he called in a thousand of his most fearsome troops from the Old Guard. The Grenadiers and the *Chasseurs à Pied* were his very best warriors, huge moustachioed men whom Napoleon had long believed in holding back to deliver the coup de grâce when his army was on the point of victory. And yet here he was committing two of their battalions to save his vulnerable flank. It was about 7.30pm. The

FRIEDRICH WILHELM VON BÜLOW

1755–1816

A devout Lutheran, General Bülow composed religious music when not commanding Prussian troops. He was forthright and short tempered, and an argument with Blücher led to his temporary retirement in 1811. Aged 60 at Waterloo, he was a veteran of the successful allied battles over the French in 1813. He defeated Marshal Ney at Dennewitz and was awarded the title Count Bülow von Dennewitz. At Waterloo, his attack on Napoleon's right flank around the village of Plancenoit produced some of the fiercest fighting of the battle. Around 6,200 of the 30,000 men he commanded in IV Corps lost their lives. When Bülow died a year later, every officer in the Prussian army wore black armbands for three days in his memory.

Old Guardsmen went about their business with a ferocity that soon had the Prussians retreating again. They rampaged through the village, fighting with bayonets and even the butts of their muskets at very close quarters. Their ruthless counter-attack was to hold off the Prussians for just one more hour – enough to give Napoleon a narrow opportunity to strike decisively elsewhere on the battlefield.

WELLINGTON'S CRISIS: THE FALL OF LA HAYE SAINTE

NO POINT ON THE BATTLEFIELD OF waterloo was more critically placed than the farm of La Haye Sainte. The struggle for it was ferocious: for five hours, a small force of Germans held it against thousands of French attackers, and its fall to Napoleon in the early evening came near to spelling disaster for Wellington. The walled compound was right in the middle of the field: it jutted forward from the centre of the allied line threatening to blunt any French attack on Wellington's main positions on the ridge. Wellington knew how vital the farm was to his defence, and he gave the task of securing it to 400 riflemen from his trusty King's German Legion. Their

Baker rifles were accurate over a far longer range than muskets, though the weapons took twice as long to load and fire.

The German light infantrymen had moved into the farm in the pouring rain the night before. Cold and wet, they looked around for fuel for a fire. In what turned out to be an unforgivable mistake, they unhinged the wooden door to the west side of the farm and fed it to the flames. Now there was nothing to stop an enemy walking in. La Haye Sainte was going to be a lot more difficult to defend than the other farmhouse at Hougoumont, and Napoleon had placed his Grand Battery of guns just

Below: British and allied squares resist French cavalry charges near the farm of La Haye Sainte. This picture illustrates the general smoke-filled confusion of the battlefield rather than one particular moment. Just below the farmhouse on the right, riflemen of the 1/95th help defend the farm, encouraged from behind by the Duke of Wellington on his horse Copenhagen. In the middle distance (centre left, riding his grey horse, Marengo) Napoleon and his mounted staff review the rest of the French army waiting in reserve.

500 metres (less than a third of a mile) away.

Astonishingly, the French guns did not target the farm. The great French opening barrage that lasted till lunchtime was aimed at the allied ridge behind La Haye Sainte. To the great relief of the farm's German commander, Major Baring, the French guns made no attempt to batter the walls of his compound. It was d'Erlon's infantry that first attacked, and Baring met them with half his force firing from behind the trees in the orchard. But the French far outnumbered them and could outshoot them too. At close range, the French were able to reload their muskets at twice the speed of the riflemen, and the Germans were soon forced to retreat to the shelter of the farm. They had to fight the French off every foot of the way and Baring's horse was shot dead under him.

A battalion of Germans from Luneburg was sent down from the ridge to reinforce Baring. However, they were spotted by French *cuirassiers* who rode in among them and left few alive. Out of 617 men, the Luneburgers lost 483 killed, wounded and missing. Colonel Ordener, the French commander of the 1st Cuirassiers, boasted later that he had "passed over" the Luneburgers: "I overthrew three officers with my own hand and their colour remained in our possession."

Somehow Baring and those of his garrison who had survived the attack on the orchard managed to scramble inside the farm and block the opening on the west side. On the other side of the farm, the big gate onto the road was slammed shut and, for the moment, the place was secured. However, the French had La Haye Sainte surrounded.

Baring's men now had to struggle to find firing positions. Because the farm's wood had been burned, they couldn't build ladders or stands to enable them to aim over the wall. However, the roof of the piggery on the east side offered a good field of fire, and they found other spots where they could bring their rifles to bear on the enemy. As d'Erlon's mass attack ran out of steam, Baring was able to receive reinforcements from the ridge. But

Above: The French stage one of many attacks on the farmhouse of La Haye Sainte, a critical outpost in front of Wellington's centre. Men of the King's German Legion (KGL) held off attackers throughout the day but by 6pm their ammunition had run out and they evacuated the farm. Here one KGL sharpshooter can be seen firing from the top of the wall and a small group (left centre) make a desperate sally against overwhelming numbers.

there was still one vital asset missing: a stock of reserve ammunition. As the afternoon wore on, Baring demanded a re-supply, but somehow his increasingly urgent pleas were either forgotten or ignored. It was, of course, more difficult to find supplies of the relatively rare balls for the Baker rifle. As the attacks carried on through the afternoon, Baring's ammunition was dwindling fast.

Napoleon was in no doubt that the storming of La Haye Sainte was essential if he was to triumph over Wellington, and he ordered Ney to waste no time in crushing Baring's resistance. With their long-range rifles, the Germans could not be allowed to remain commanding a position from which they could threaten the flanks of any attack on Wellington's main line on the ridge. Ney mounted a number of attacks throughout the afternoon, but again the great line of guns remained blind to the opportunity that the farm's walls offered. Napoleon's 12-pounders could have blasted a hole in the walls and they would certainly have battered down the large gate onto the road. However, the gate and the walls remained intact.

At 3pm and again at 5pm, thousands of French infantry attempted to carry the battle into the farm's courtyard without success. After the first assault, 17 Frenchmen lay dead in the gap where the western door had been torn away by the Germans the night before. The pile of corpses served as a barricade that the French failed to break through. In the second attack, the French did manage to set light to the barn. Baring was lucky that a unit of reinforcing Germans from the state of Nassau had brought camp kettles with them: they used these to carry water from the farm's pond to douse the flames. But the Nassauers, who were armed with muskets, had not brought with them any of the vital rifle ammunition that Baring's men desperately needed. Baring sent a final appeal for ammunition. He warned that without it, he would have to abandon the position. None arrived. Wellington later said that failing to supply Baring was one of the worst mistakes

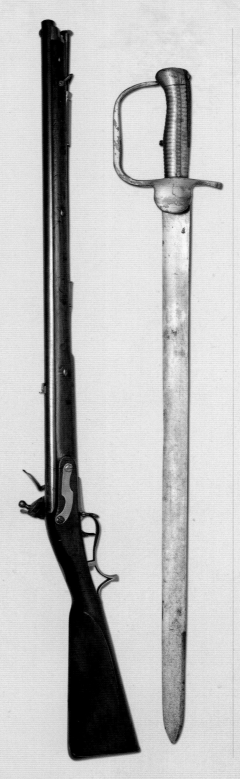

Left: A Baker rifle and its sword bayonet. Still relatively new to warfare, this weapon was a breakthrough in small arms development. Its rifled barrel - unlike the smooth-bore musket carried by most soldiers - allowed sharpshooters in the light infantry to hit targets at far greater range. The rifle took longer to load but had around four times the range of the musket.

CHRISTIAN FRIEDRICH WILHEM VON OMPTEDA
1765–1815

Of Ompteda's final moments, one eyewitness wrote, "So he died – a man of noble soul, distinguished in mind and character… a hero's death." Ompteda joined the army aged 16 and was one of the first members of the Kings's German Legion. At Waterloo, he objected to his divisional commander General Alten's order to attack La Haye Sainte only to be overruled by the Prince of Orange. He begged a colleague to take care of his two young teenage nephews in the regiment, and then led his men towards the farmhouse. Shot in the neck at close range, he is buried in a mass grave on the battlefield.

made at Waterloo.

When the next attack struck him shortly after 6pm and Baring knew that his riflemen were down to their last two or three rounds, he reluctantly decided that he would have to withdraw his men as best he could. There was only one way out – through the farmhouse at the north end of the courtyard and out through the kitchen garden at the back. As his men pulled back, the French poured into the courtyard. There was fierce hand-to-hand fighting as Baring's men scrambled through the narrow passageway of the house and out of the back door into the vegetable garden. Some men were cut down while others tried to hide. One young soldier, an ensign named Franks, hid under a bed. He heard comrades being bayoneted where they were hiding in the same room, but was astonished to be left alone. He was lucky. Only 42 of Baring's original 400 escaped from La Haye Sainte alive and made it to the top of the ridge, a few hundred yards behind, where they and their exemplary commander collapsed exhausted behind the allied lines. Within moments, the French had occupied the farm.

No sooner was it clear that the farm had fallen into French hands than a futile effort was made to repossess it. Baring's brigade commander, Colonel Ompteda, was horrified to receive an order from his overall commander, the Dutch Prince of Orange, to lead a battalion in an attempt to recapture it. Ompteda – who knew the action would almost certainly end in failure – nevertheless felt duty-bound to lead his men in an attack. Ompteda charged in way ahead of his men and, to the admiration of the French – who for a moment stood by without firing at him – threw himself into the fray and went down fighting. Minutes later, French heavy artillery was rushed up to the front, past La Haye Sainte and up to a point just north of the farm, where it could fire almost point blank into the allied lines. The 27th infantry regiment, the Inniskillings, were crowded into a small area just beyond the brow of the hill. They were almost totally destroyed by the gunfire.

The French advance, Ompteda's sacrifice and the destruction of the 27th now left Wellington's centre dangerously exposed. Aware that this was his moment of greatest crisis, Wellington rode along the front working meticulously to fill the gaps. Miraculously, he escaped being hit. These were anxious moments. It was 6.30pm; the balance of the battle of Waterloo had shifted momentarily in Napoleon's favour and Marshal Ney knew it. If he could persuade the Emperor to give him enough troops, he believed he could deliver France the victory.

Overleaf: The storming of La Haye Sainte. The French smash through the defences of this vital farmhouse at 6pm. Major Baring (mounted with sword outstretched in the centre) urges his men to resist as best they can. But in the end, with ammunition running low, they have to abandon the farm.

THE CHARGE AND REPULSE OF THE IMPERIAL GUARD

WITH LA HAYE SAINTE IN FRENCH hands and his artillery now close enough to the ridge to cause havoc in Wellington's centre, Ney made an urgent appeal to Napoleon. If the Emperor could provide him with troops to allow him to strike immediately, he could deliver the decisive blow.

"Troops?" asked Napoleon. "Where do you expect to me to get any troops from? Do you expect me to make them?" Ney's appeal had come at a bleak moment for Napoleon, whose eyes were on the battle with the Prussians over to his right. He had taken the agonizing decision to dig into his precious final reserve – the Old Guard – and commit two of its battalions to the fight with Blücher. Only when he knew they had succeeded in beating back the Prussians and buying him a little extra time, did he feel able to turn back to Wellington. If he had reinforced Ney at around 6.30pm, Wellington would have been caught at his most vulnerable moment. However, an hour later, Wellington was able to shift forces on his left – now replaced by Ziethen's Prussians – across to strengthen his centre. The French had lost a major opportunity.

Left: Short-tailed coatee worn during the Waterloo campaign by Lieutenant Henry Anderson.of the 2nd battalion the 69th (South Lincolnshire) regiment. A tear in the jacket (top right) shows where Anderson was wounded in the shoulder.

Overleaf: The attack of the Imperial Guard. Napoleon watches the massed squares of his Old and Middle Guard marching up the slope towards the red-coated British Guards battalions on the opposite slope. It is his last desperate effort to break through Wellington's line.

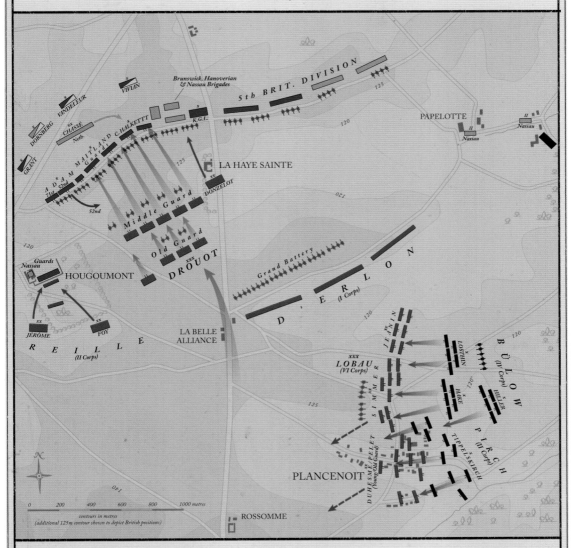

THE IMPERIAL GUARD ATTACK AND THE PRUSSIAN BREAKTHROUGH
7.30PM, 18 JUNE 1815

—6—

Brunswick, Hanoverian & Nassau Brigades

5th BRIT. DIVISION

DORNBERG

VANDELEUR

VIVIAN

CHASSÉ
Neth.

C. HALKETT

K.G.L.

PAPELOTTE

Nassau

Nassau

GRANT

MAITLAND
Guds

AD M
71st 52nd

52nd

LA HAYE SAINTE

DONZELOT

Middle Guard

Old Guard

Grand Battery

D'ERLON

Guards
Nassau

HOUGOUMONT

DROUOT

D'ERLON
(I Corps)

REILLE
(II Corps)

JERÔME

FOY

LA BELLE
ALLIANCE

JELININ

LOSTHIN

HILLER

BÜLOW
(IV Corps)

LOBAU
(VI Corps)

SIMMER

HAKE

PLANCENOIT

DUHESME PELET
(Young Old Guard)

TIPPELSKIRCH

PIRCH
(II Corps)

N

0 200 400 600 800 1000 metres

contours in metres
(additional 125m contour shown to depict British positions)

ROSSOMME

AROUND 7.30PM NAPOLEON ORDERS the Imperial Guard to attack Wellington's right. Five Middle Guard battalions advance up the slope with four more battalions in reserve behind them.

Colin Halkett's brigade, which is under heavy pressure, is rescued by Chassé's Dutch-Belgians.

The attack on Maitland's Guards prompts Adam to move his 52nd forward and swing left to attack the flank of the Imperial Guard's assault.

The Imperial Guard retreats under overwhelming British fire.

The Prussian corps of Pirch and Bülow, now heavily reinforced by Blücher, force Lobau and his Imperial Guard reinforcements to withdraw from Plancenoit.

JOHN COLBORNE
1778–1863

Unlike many of Wellington's commanders, Colborne did not buy his way to the top. His rise through the ranks was due to hard work and talent. He fought in most of the Peninsular War battles and was badly injured in the Siege of Ciudad Rodrigo in 1812. After Napoleon's return from Elba, it was Colborne who convinced the British Prince Regent not to attack the French army until Wellington had arrived. In 1828, Colborne became Lieutenant Governor of Upper Canada, founding the still-famous Upper Canada College. After serving as Governor General of British North America, Colborne was honoured with the title 1st Baron Seaton.

However, Napoleon decided to make a final desperate throw of the dice. He knew that if he failed to defeat Wellington, he would face overwhelming odds once the Russians and Austrians moved up to join the allies. Victory at Waterloo would massively improve his chances of achieving his strategic aim of defeating his opponents one by one. It was worth one last effort to snatch that victory. In a gamble typical of the man who throughout has career had played for the highest stakes, Napoleon dismissed the option of an ordered withdrawal. Instead of retaining the main body of his Imperial Guard to cover a retreat, he ordered nine of its remaining battalions to move forward under his personal command and prepare to assault Wellington's centre right.

The allies had warning of the Imperial Guard's attack. A little earlier, a French *cuirassier* colonel had ridden forward waving his sword above his head and shouting, "*Vive le Roi*, Long Live the King!" Utterly disillusioned by the futility of the great French cavalry charges, he had deserted. And he brought news that Napoleon had decided to commit the Imperial Guard.

Soon after 7.30pm, around 6,000 men of the Guard advanced up the slope between La Haye Sainte and Hougoumont supported by their horse artillery. They were fresh into the

battle, fiercely motivated and buoyed up by the false report that Grouchy had returned. The attack was led by five Middle Guard battalions and backed up by one Middle Guard battalion and three Old Guard battalions in reserve. Napoleon handed over command to Ney as they passed La Haye Sainte. Each battalion adopted the form of a square as it moved up the slope: it meant that not all their muskets could be brought to bear as they approached the enemy, but they would be protected against cavalry. Their years of training would keep their formations intact.

The advancing battalions made an astonishing sight. Drums beating, the 3,000 men in the lead tramped up through the corn which had largely been flattened by the earlier cavalry charges. They had to weave their way up a slope littered with dead and wounded men and horses. Wellington's troops waiting in lines – four men deep – behind the ridge watched them appear over the brow "in splendid order". As one witness wrote, "… as they rose step by step before us… they loomed most formidably, and when I thought of their character, and saw their noble bearing, I certainly thought we were in for very slashing work."

Waiting to meet the assault were two brigades consisting of British troops. One of them was – for a moment – to come close to

Below: Medal of the Legion of Honour for a Chevalier (5th class), inscribed *Honneur et Patrie*. Said to have been taken from the dead body of a colonel in the Imperial Guard at Waterloo.

collapse. As the Imperial Guard tramped into view, the 5th Brigade's commander, Major-General Sir Colin Halkett, ordered his men to fire a volley. The Guard, shocked by its impact, halted and returned fire. The defenders, most of them inexperienced recruits and unprotected by any artillery, were seen by the French to pull back. And with Halkett himself suddenly wounded by a ball that passed through his face – in one cheek and out the other – there was desperate confusion as the regiments became tangled up. One officer remarked that if the French had sent in 50 *cuirassiers*, "they would have annihilated our brigade". Once again Wellington's line was in danger of being broken.

Few British soldiers regarded the Dutch-Belgians with much trust or respect. But their intervention at this dramatic moment helped to turn the battle against the Imperial Guard. Wellington had placed them in a second line behind Halkett's men. Their appearance on the ridge beside the British commander's faltering units accompanied by a battery of Dutch gunners firing lethal case shot helped to turn the tide. Under a withering fire from the fast rallying British line, the Guard retreated down the hill.

Halkett's line had survived. The other brigade, the British Guards, did more than survive – they decisively turned the tide of battle. Wellington had his 1,500 guardsmen – commanded by Major-General Peregrine Maitland – lie down behind the brow of the hill out of sight of the two regiments of the French *Chasseurs à Pied* approaching up the incline to their front. Maitland's men, like Halkett's, were in lines, every musket ready to bear on the enemy. And when the Imperial Guardsmen appeared as little as 27 metres (89 feet) away to their front, Wellington shouted, "Now Maitland! Now's your time!" The order was given, the men were on their feet with bayonets fixed, and a massive volley rang out.

The effect of the initial allied volley was shattering. Napoleon's Imperial Guard shuddered to a halt as great gaps appeared in the front ranks. Men falling dead or wounded cluttered the ground and impeded the progress of the others. Within seconds, Imperial Guardsmen still on their feet faced a bayonet charge. Smoke was everywhere and the din was appalling. The screams of

Below: Wellington on his chestnut stallion Copenhagen during the final moments at Waterloo. When he saw the final French collapse and retreat he is reported to have raised his arm and exclaimed: "Forward and complete your victory."

the wounded mixed with the defiant cries of those charging at each other on either side. Some ranks of the French quickly recovered from the initial shock and resumed their momentum. The battle hung in the balance. Ney was somewhere in the front rank of the Imperial Guard. He had lost five horses killed under him that day. Now he was on foot among the men, slashing about with his sword. He was heard to shout to one colleague, "We must die here."

On the extreme right of the British line, the 52nd Light Infantry, around 1,000 strong, stood just beyond the reach of the French assault. The regiment's commander, Colonel John Colborne – who had led many a triumph in the Peninsular War – saw an opportunity to bring deadly fire on the French attackers. He led his battalion into the empty ground ahead and swung them to the left in a long line facing the flank of the Imperial Guard. Then they loosed off volley after volley into the French sweeping across their front. The 4th regiment of the *Chasseurs à Pied* were cut down rank after rank.

Below: General Chassé's Dutch-Belgians storm to the rescue at the climax of the final phase of Waterloo. Colin Halkett's brigade are under huge pressure from Napoleon's Imperial Guard and their allies come to their aid in the nick of time.

Colborne's volleys from the flank and the well-drilled steadiness of the two Guards battalions were too much for the Chasseurs of the Middle Guard. They no longer had the strength or the will to press on forward. They turned and retreated down the hill. All five of the squares began to break up into groups of men withdrawing the way they had approached. The cry of *"La Garde recule!"* echoed through the ranks of the rest of the French army as it watched in astonished horror. The cry was soon followed by a shout from the retreating troops: *"Sauve qui peut!"* – "Every man for himself".

Wellington was quick to see an opportunity. He had seen before the speed at which the spectre of defeat could be transformed into victory. Rather than watch the enemy withdraw in its own time, he was heard – according to one account – to mutter to himself, "Oh damn it! In for a penny, in for a pound!" Then he raised his hat above his head and ordered his entire army forward. He rode along the whole front line urging his men to advance in pursuit. And when one group of men roared their approval, he responded coolly, "No cheering lads, but forward and complete your victory!"

Below: British guardsmen counter charge the assault by Napoleon's Imperial Guard at the climax of the battle. Some of the French are already turning in flight. Note the bushy mustachios the British artist has given the French guardsmen.

PRIVATE JOHN ABBOTT

12 NOVEMBER 1815

An extract from a letter from Private John Abbott of the 51st Regiment to Miss Anne Banks on 12 November 1815.

"There was whole regiments cut down, and not a charge of the Imperial Guard was entirely destroyed."

"I Take this most Pleasing opportunity of Sending these few Lines to you Still hoping to find you and All Friends well as this leaves us Both very well In health and Spirits at present thank God for all his Mercies[.] My Dr Friend we may properlly think of his Great Mercies after Escaping such a Tremendous Battle which Partly I will relate To You. But theres one Thing to remark you don't properly understand the miserable Nature of a Battle when I First Left home I had verry Little Idea of Seeing So many of my fellow Creatures Destroyd By the Dreadful Sword ..."

Venice Novr — 12th — 1815

Dr "Ann

Take this most Pleasing opportuni
ty Of Sending these few Lines to You Still
hoping to find You and All friends well
as this Leaves Us Both very well In Heal
th and Spirits at present Thank God for all
his Mercies My Dr Friend as may futurely
think Of This Great Mercies after Escaping such
a Tremenduous Battle which Partly I will relate
To You But theres one thing to remark you dont
properly Understand the Miserable Nature of
a Battle when I first Left home I had very
Little Idea of Seeing So many of My fellow
Creatures Destroyd By the Dreadful (Sword) when
first Napoleon — Made his Escape from the Island
of Elba he Made the Best of his Way for the
Grand City of Paris and of Course Louis the
18th Was Oblig to Fly making his way for holland
where he was Under the Protection of the Prince

Of Orange and Immediately Orders was Dispatch
to the Different Allied Powers we Lay in Portsmouth
and Embark'd Immediately for Ostend a Place in
French Flanders we Arived there in 24 hours and
then Embark'd in their Canal Boats and proceded
to the Famous City of Ghent a Town in the
Lower Netherlands where Louis the Present King
of France was and the unmarkable Civill reseption
we Received there Exceded any Kind Treatment
and then we Suddenly we Departed By
orders and march'd for a Place Call Grammown a
Town in the Upper Netherlands all In Holland there
we remain 10 Weeks and we were as happy as Ever
I was In My Life But Every day our Army
was preparing the Unfortunate Implements of war and
It is dreadfull that Mankind Should make destruction for
one Another End But it fullfills the Scripture
All Suddenly a Prussian Dragoon Arive At Break
of day on the Morning of the 16th of June with Information to the Duke of Wellington that Napoleon and his
Army was Rapidly Advancing with 175 Thousand Men
on the City of Brussells and that the Prussians and

A Few English Troops had Been Sharply Engaged and Severely Beatten By the French and So they were and a Number Killd But Behold your Lord Wellington was not there But our Bugle Horns Sounded the Alarm and we prepare for attatching Napoleon and Marshall Seauts from the French from their further Progress and on the Evening of the 17th we arrived in Front of the Enemy 55 thousand only against 75 thousand and At 10 OClock on the 18th Wellington received A Challenge from Bonaparte and certainly Excepted of It and precisely at Noon the Engagement Began and from that Untill 8 that Night Never one moment ceased Slaughtering Each other there has not A Laid Contested Battle since the great Storm the French fought very hard and very obstinate Never Gave Us one Inch Of Ground nor we them there was whole regiments Cut to Piees at a Charge the French Imperial Guards was Entirely Destroyd it Began Going very hard with the English 3 OClock in the Afternoon But the Almighty assist us and the whole English declare to Wellington that they would die to their Last Man our General when he find a firm resolution we fix our Bayonetts and Gave the Proud Monsieurs Such a dressing as the will ever thinke of about 8 OClock in the Evening the Prussians Made their Appearance and a little after the Whole French Army runaway we pursue and on the 24th of June we come Up to them at a City Call Cambray where we once More Trouble them we then Pursued to Paris where we Soon Tooke their whole Nations and My Dear at Present we are as happy as the Day Is Long

IMPERIAL GUARD PAYBOOK

Paybook of a French soldier of the Imperial Guard recovered from the battlefield at Waterloo. The printed section at the back lists the penalties soldiers face for various misdemeanours, ranging from one month in prison for a general unauthorized absence, to death for speaking to the enemy without permission. Other punishments included fers (mettre aux fers) – to be put in irons, boulet (boulet et bagnard) – ball and chain, and trav pub (travaux publics) – a cross between hard labour and community service.

EFFETS DE LINGE ET CHAUSSURE.

DESIGNATION DES EFFETS.	Quantités que doit avoir un S.r Offic. ou Soldat.	ÉPOQUES DES REVUES ET QUANTITÉS.			
		Du 1.er janvier 181	Du 1.er	Du 1.er	Du 1.er
Chemises		2	2		
Pantalon de toile					
Cols { noirs		1	1		
{ blancs . . .			1		
Mouchoirs de poche . .					
Paires de { de fil ou coton					
bas . . . { de laine . .	1				
Paires de souliers	3	2	2		
Paires de { grises		1	1		
guêtres. { noires d'étoffe	1				
Sacs. { de toile . . .	1	1	1		
{ de peau . . .		1	1		
Cocardes		1	1		
Pompon					
Plumet					
Boucles					
Couvre-giberne		1	1		
Tournevis		1	1		
Tire-balle		1	1		
Epinglette			1		
Bouteille clissée					

COMPTE COURANT.

DATES.	OBJETS DES RECETTES ET DÉPENSES.	RECETTES.		DÉPENSES.	
		fr.	c.	fr.	c.
	d'entrée d'art . .	6	88	16	50
	produit du 1.er 9.bre	9			
	Dépense	"	"		
	recette	15	88	16	50
				15	88
	Paris reû doit . . .	"	"	"	62
	Le Cap.ne D.e du Cang.t				
	Ferraty				

NOMENCLATURE ALPHABÉTIQUE DES DÉLITS MILITAIRES
et Peines y attachées.

DÉLITS.	PEINES.
Abandon de son poste pour se livrer au pillage.	Fers, 5 ans.
Abandon de voitures.	Mort.
Absence à la générale.	Prison, 1 mois.
Absence à la générale avec récidive.	Prison, 6 mois.
Absence à la générale pour la troisième fois.	Fers, 2 ans.
Absence avec récidive lorsqu'on marche à l'ennemi.	Fers, 2 ans.
Assassinat pour fuir.	Mort.
Attroupement (chef d').	Fers, 5 ans.
Attroupement (auteur d').	Mort.
Bons (fabrication de faux).	Fers, 5 ans.
Changement de consigne proche l'ennemi.	Prison, 6 mois.
Clameurs séditieuses.	Mort.
Complot de désertion.	Mort.
Congé falsifié.	Fers, 5 ans.
Consigne changée près l'enn. sans en rendre compte.	Prison, 6 mois.
Consigne fausse compromettant la sûreté.	Mort.
Consigne forcée à l'armée.	Fers, 10 ans.
Consigne non exécutée proche l'ennemi.	Fers, 2 ans.
Correspondance avec l'ennemi sans permission.	Mort.
Dépouillement d'un mort sans ordre.	Fers, 5 ans.
Dépouillement d'un vivant.	Mort.
Désertion à l'intérieur.	Trav. publ., 3 ans.
Désertion avec récidive.	Mort.
Désertion de l'armée ou d'une place de première lig.	Trav. publ., 5 ans.
Désertion d'un suppléant.	Boulet, 5 ans.
Désertion de service ou par-dessus le rempart.	Trav. publ., 5 ans.
Désertion avec effets de l'état ou du corps.	Trav. publ., 5 ans.
Désertion avec effets de ses camarades.	Boulet, 10 ans.
Désertion à l'intérieur non individuelle.	Trav. publ., 5 ans.
Désertion à l'étranger.	Mort.
Désertion à l'étranger.	Boulet, 10 ans.
Désertion à l'étranger avec récidive ou de service.	Mort.
Désertion après amnistie.	Mort.
Désertion après grace.	Mort.
Désertion avec armes à feu.	Mort.
Désertion des travaux publics.	Boulet, 10 ans.
Désertion du chef de complot.	Mort.
Désertion en faction.	Mort.
Désertion de toute espèce (outre la peine).	Amende de 1500 fr.
Désobéissance combinée.	Mort.
Désobéissance d'une troupe (chefs de)	Fers, 10 ans.
Désobéissance en face de l'ennemi.	Mort.
Distraction d'habillement.	Fers, 5 ans.
Double paye.	Destit. et amende.
Embauchage.	Mort.
Enclouage du canon sans ordre.	Fers, 3 ans.
Enlèvement d'un détenu.	Fers, 5 ans.
Enrôlement double.	Mort.
Espionnage.	Mort.

DÉLITS.	PEINES.
Évasion des prisonniers de guerre.	Fers, 6 ans.
Falsification de congé.	Fers, 5 ans.
Falsification de consigne compromettant le poste.	Mort.
Fauteur de désertion.	Prison, 1 an.
Faux témoignage causant la mort.	Mort.
Faux certificat de la maladie.	Fers, 2 ans.
Fraude chez un habitant.	Prison, 3 mois.
Fraude avec menaces.	Prison, 6 mois.
Fraude avec voie de fait.	Fers, 2 ans.
Fuite des prisonniers de guerre.	Fers, 6 ans.
Gage (mise d'effets ou armes).	Fers, 5 ans.
Incendie.	Mort.
Infidélité dans le poids des rations.	Fers, 2 ans.
Infidélité dans les états de troupe.	Fers, 5 ans.
Inscription sous un faux nom.	Fers, 5 ans.
Insulte à une sentinelle.	Prison, 2 ans.
Insulte avec voie de fait.	Mort.
Insulte par le subordonné avec propos ou geste.	Fers, 5 ans.
Insulte par le subordonné avec voie de fait.	Mort.
Lâcheté en faction en présence de l'ennemi.	Mort.
Lâcheté par abandon de ses armes dans une affaire.	Fers, 2 ans.
Manque à sa consigne près l'ennemi.	Exposition.
Maraude.	Fers, 5 ans.
Maraude avec persistance ou récidive.	Fers, 5 ans.
Maraude d'une troupe armée.	Fers, 8 ans.
Menaces du subordonné.	Fers, 5 ans.
Menaces avec voie de fait.	Mort.
Mutinerie des prisonniers de guerre.	Mort.
Pillage à main armée.	Mort.
Réception d'un déserteur au camp après la retraite.	Fers, 5 ans.
Refus de l'emploi de la force.	Détention, 3 ans.
Refus formel de marcher à l'ennemi.	Mort.
Résistance des prisonniers de guerre.	Mort.
Révélation à l'ennemi du mot d'ordre.	Mort.
Service contre la France.	Mort.
Sommeil d'un factionnaire près l'ennemi.	Fers, 5 ans.
Substitution de nom sur un congé.	Mort.
Trahison.	Mort.
Trompette qui, sans ordre, passe les avant-postes.	Fers, 5 ans.
Vente d'armes, habillemens ou équipemens.	Fers, 5 ans.
Viol.	Fers, 8 ans.
Viol d'une fille de moins de 14 ans.	Fers, 12 ans.
Viol suivi de mort.	Mort.
Violation de la consigne générale.	Fers, 10 ans.
Vol chez son hôte.	Fers, 10 ans.
Vol envers ses camarades.	Fers, 6 ans.
Vol de poudre ou autres munitions.	Fers, 3 ans.
Vol en augmentant l'effectif de la troupe.	Fers, 3 ans.
Vol de fournitures de caserne.	Fers, 5 ans.
Voie de fait envers le subordonné.	Prison, 1 an.
Voie de fait du subordonné envers le chef.	Mort.
Usage du congé d'autrui.	Fers, 5 ans.

THE FRENCH ROUT
AND THE
HUMAN COSTS

A S WELLINGTON WATCHED HIS men charge down the hill, his cavalry commander, Lord Uxbridge, was at his side. Uxbridge was the man who had led the heavy cavalry charge that had scattered d'Erlon's infantry earlier in the day; he was now eager to lead what was left of Wellington's horsemen into the final battle. But before he could dig his spurs into his mount, a French canister shot shattered his leg. Uxbridge famously told the duke, "By God, I have lost my leg!"

"By God, sir," replied the duke, removing his telescope from his eye. "So you have!" Wellington instantly arranged for Uxbridge and his favourite aide, the severely wounded Colonel Sir Alexander Gordon, to be given immediate medical care at his headquarters in the village of Waterloo.

Within minutes of the British and their allies driving the defeated French before them, the Prussians broke through at Plancenoit and joined the pursuit. Blücher's chief of staff, General Gneisenau, led the

Below: Prussian troops overrun the cemetery at Plancenoit. Napoleon has sent in part of his Imperial Guard in a desperate bid to save the village and shore up his right wing. But the Prussians outnumber them and eventually throw them back.

Left: A study by George Jones for his *The Battle of Waterloo* painting, 1815. This study shows a Highlander of the Black Watch attending a wounded General of Hussars, possibly Lord Uxbridge.

Overleaf: General Lord Hill calls on the remnant of Napoleon's Imperial Guard to surrender. Most of the Guard, together with the rest of the defeated French army, are in full flight pursued by the Prussians.

furious Prussians in what fast became a merciless crusade of revenge for what they had suffered at the hands of the French that day and in the years since 1806. By the late evening, the Prussians had taken over the entire chase. They stopped at nothing and took very few prisoners. Frenchmen they caught up with – even the wounded – were bayoneted. One British officer noticed a British cavalryman about to be killed by the Prussians and shouted, *"Er ist ein Englander!"* – "He is an Englishman!" He just managed to save him.

One French officer described the scene as one of utter panic. Entire French units flung their weapons away and knelt down crying *"pardon"* in the forlorn hope that they might be spared: "There was nothing more than a confused mass of infantry cavalry and guns that rushed... like an unstoppable torrent. ... Alone several squares of the Guard remained immobile as rocks in a raging sea."

The four squares of guardsmen that Napoleon had intended to form the second wave of the assault on the ridge were the only French battalions left to maintain order. The guardsmen found themselves having to shoot dead groups of frantic French fugitives as they struggled to break into the squares for safety. Several attacks were made on the squares, but the British failed to break them up. Only when one Imperial Guard commander, General Cambronne, found himself suddenly outside his square, did the British pounce and make him captive. He was the man credited with the proud boast, *"La Garde meurt mais ne se rend pas!"* – "The Guard dies but does not surrender!" Cambronne later denied he had ever said this and claimed – as the story goes – he had merely uttered a single word, *"Merde!"* – "Shit!"

Few, if any, other French units remained intact. British light dragoons slashing their

way through the retreating enemy saw no sign of the dreaded *cuirassiers*, though they found themselves picking their way through a clutter of discarded *cuirasses*.

An exhausted Napoleon initially sought refuge in one of the squares, then climbed into his coach and was driven to Genappe. But the street there was very congested and, with the Prussians hot on his trail, Napoleon leapt on his horse and rode off to the French border late that night. When the Prussians caught up with the beleaguered carriages abandoned by Napoleon and his top staff, they seized the Emperor's private fortune of gold coins and diamonds hidden in his coach.

With their victory assured, Wellington and Blücher met at a farm neatly called "La Belle Alliance". As they shook hands,

Above: Dutch-Belgian and Prussian troops meet near Maison du Roi, on the evening of 18 June 1815, after the battle. Painting by John Hoynck van Papendrecht.

HARRY SMITH
1787–1860

Captain Harry Smith had an extraordinary career. He served in the Peninsular War and in the War of 1812 with America, where he was present at the burning of the White House in 1814. He returned in time for Waterloo and later served in India. He proposed to a 14-year-old girl from a noble Spanish family minutes after rescuing her from marauding British troops at the siege of Badajoz in 1812. As his wife, Juana followed Smith loyally from battle to battle, and he called her his "guardian angel". Later, General Sir Harry Smith, accompanied by Lady Juana, became Governor of the Cape. The South Africans named two towns after them – Harrismith and Ladysmith.

Blücher said, *"Mein lieber kamerad, quelle affaire!"* Wellington later remarked that these were the only two French words Blücher was capable of. But in his despatch to the British government, Wellington made no secret of his debt to the Prussians: "I should not do justice to my feelings or to Marshal Blücher and the Prussians if I did not attribute the successful result of this arduous day to the cordial and timely assistance I received from them."

As darkness fell, the battlefield was a ghastly sight. Men and horses lay everywhere. There were up to 45,000 dead and wounded – half of this number being French. Many couldn't leave the field and little effort was made to reach them that night. Men who were unable to move had to endure not only the pain and the cold, but also the pitiless attention of scavengers who snatched or tore off them any item of the slightest value. Many men were left naked. Robbing the dead was easy, while any wounded who remonstrated were easily despatched with a pistol or dagger. Soldiers looking for loot occasionally refrained from stripping the corpses of their own side, but penniless Belgian peasants on the prowl had no such scruples. From shoes full of holes to torn tunics, anything that was thought worth stealing was taken. One surviving soldier was so hungry that he grabbed a piece of bread lying in the open haversack of a comrade who had been shot in the head. He had to scrape the man's brains off the loaf with his pocket-knife before he could eat it.

The smell of the corpses and the groans of the dying and wounded added to the horror. The din was punctuated every now and then by the pistol shots of those who took pity on the wounded horses or the hammering of blacksmiths stripping dead animals of their horseshoes. It took up to 12 days to clear the battlefield. The bodies were thrown into trenches that held around 40 corpses each.

One of the most mournful sights was that of friends and relatives anxiously searching the battlefield for loved ones. The wife of one of Wellington's staff officers, Major Harry Smith, had the harrowing experience of being told that a Major Harry Smith had been killed. She then spent some time desperately searching for his body only to discover a little later that the dead man

Below: The Duke of Wellington meets Field Marshal Blücher after their victory at a house called La Belle Alliance. Wellington had every reason to be grateful to Blücher, who had committed some 50,000 troops by the end of the battle.

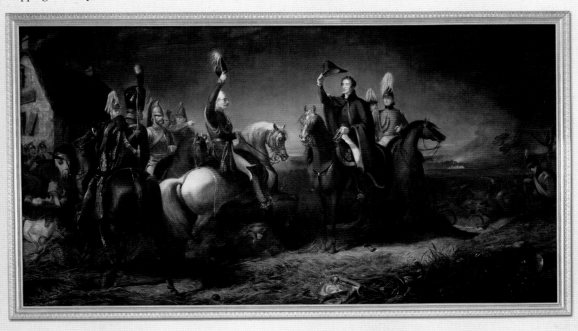

was her husband's namesake. The Harry Smith whom she had married three years earlier in Spain during the Peninsular War – and faithfully followed from battlefield to battlefield – was, after all, safe and sound.

The wounded – such as Lord Uxbridge and Frederick Ponsonby, who had both been severely injured in the cavalry charges – were lucky if they survived the primitive medical treatment of the time. There were no antibiotics, no anaesthetics and no sophisticated medicines. The likeliest treatment for a musket ball in the arm or leg was an amputation, the only sure way to stop death from lead poisoning. Victims would have to make do with a glass of brandy and a leather strap to bite on as the limb was sawn off. Uxbridge's bravery under the surgeon's knife soon became legendary. He was told he risked death if he didn't have the leg sawn off. "If it's to come off, then the sooner it's done the better," he replied. He never complained during the operation, but remained cool and calm. His aide-de-camp noted that his pulse remained steady throughout. His leg was afterwards buried with due honours in the garden.

As Napoleon rode on towards Paris with the Prussians in pursuit, Wellington returned to his quarters in the village of

Below: The morning after Waterloo. Around 45,000 men and countless horses lie dead, dying or severely wounded on the battlefield. Many are from Wellington's army and those of his allies. "Next to a battle lost", he said later, "the greatest misery is a battle gained."

Waterloo. He ate and slept briefly, and then early on the morning of 19 June he wrote his account of the battle, which was to reach the British government two days later.

His Waterloo despatch was written in typical Wellington style – simply stated and without embroidery: "We maintained our position... and completely defeated and repulsed all the enemy's attempts to get possession of it. The enemy repeatedly attacked us with a large body of cavalry and infantry supported by a numerous and powerful artillery; he made several charges with the cavalry upon our infantry but all were repulsed in the steadiest manner.... It gives me great pleasure", he continued, "to assure your Lordship that the army never, upon any occasion, conducted itself better." Wellington praised a number – though not all – of his senior officers, including Uxbridge, Picton and Maitland, as well as warmly crediting Blücher and the Prussians.

The only bit of conceit that Wellington allowed himself in his description of the battle was in a remark he later made to a friend. He said that Waterloo was "the nearest run thing you ever saw in your life. By God! I don't think it would have done if I had not been there." He was almost certainly right.

LIEUTENANT-COLONEL HENRY MURRAY

JOURNAL 18 JUNE 1815

Journal of the campaign written by Lieutenant-Colonel the Honourable Henry Murray of the 18th Hussars; he makes additional comments in the margins, which are transcribed here in square brackets, alongside the original entry.

18th June 1815. The morning had improved when the Brigade moved down to its position – that was on the left of the line. The ground was extremely deep – & the fine standing corn was lamentably trodden down.

The Action commencing the Brigade was in a short time exposed to Cannonade attended with little or no loss, though the fire was frequent.

The prevailing fire was towards the centre of the Armies & to our right – as heavy as possible.

So far as the movements of the enemy were discoverable to us on our Regimental Posts, the enemy's main pressure was on the centre. Sir Hussey Vivian at this time had ridden forward so as to have a better view of the Battle. A Prussian Officer came with the intelligence of the advance of that army.

& after some lapse of time Major Honble Henry Percy one of the Duke of Wellington's Aid de Camps came to ascertain how soon the Prussians might be expected.

Moving then to our right the day was clearer, we had but little if any interruption from fire ourselves, while at the same time a much better view opened to us of the features of the action.

Like the army of Xerxes the French pressed on in the Centre

a dense & countless column.

[From Major Percy we heard of the fall of Sir Wm Ponsonby & of the wound of Col. Frederick Ponsonby. Subsequently we heard of the wound of Col Hay 16th Lt Drag^s when we joined for a time General Vandeleur's Brigade.]

Continuing to move to the right we joined for a time General Vandeleur's Brigade. – Moving again to & to the rear-ward to pass a little copse we proceeded still more to the right. Colonel Quentin was shortly afterwards wounded.

The Brigade now began to tread the ground of devastation, the pavement of the main Brussells Chaussée was torn up and scattered.

Lord Edward Somerset's Brigade was formed, dwindled to a various Squadron: General Vivian asked "Lord Edward where is your Brigade?" "Here" said Lord Edward. – The Ground was strewed with wounded over whom it was hardly possible sometimes to avoid moving. Wounded or mutilated horses wandered or turned in circles – the noise was deafening & the air of ruin & destruction that prevailed wherever the eye could reach gave nothing of the exhilaration of victory. Lord Uxbridge in Hussar uniform mounted on a common troop horse (his own being exhausted) rode with General Vivian a short time in our front. Colonel Sir Felton Harvey came to exchange his wounded horse – & in the act of mounting a Troop horse of the 18th exclaimed "Lord Wellington has won the Battle if we could but get the d—d to advance." then galloped to the front.

June 1815.

The morning had improved when the Brigade moved
down to its position — that was on the left of the line.
The ground was extremely deep - & the fine standing
corn was lamentably trodden down.
The action commencing the Brigade was in a
short time exposed to cannonade attended with little
or no loss, though the fire was frequent.
The prevailing fire was towards the centre of the
armies & to our right - as heavy as possible.
So far as the movements of the enemy were discoverable
to us on our Regimental Posts, the enemy's main pressure
was on the centre. Sir Hussey Vivian at this time had
ridden forward so as to have a better view of the Battle.
A Prussian officer came with the intelligence of the advance of that army.
& after some lapse of time Major Hon.ble Henry Percy one of the
Duke of Wellington's aid de camps came to ascertain how
soon the Prussians might be expected

moving then to our right, the day was clearer, we had
but little if any interruption from fire ourselves, while
at the same time a much better view opened to us of the
features of the action.
Like the army of Xerxes the French pressed on in the
centre a dense & countless column.
continuing to move to the right - we joined for a time
General Vandeleur's Brigade. ... moving again
& to the rear-ward to pass a little copse we proceeded
still more to the right. Colonel Quentin was shortly
afterwards wounded.
The Brigade now began to tread the ground of devastation, the pavement of the main Brussels thoroughfare
was torn up & scattered.
Lord Edward Somerset's Brigade was formed, divided
into various squadron: General Vivian asked
"Lord Edward where is your Brigade?" "Here" said Lord
Edward. — The ground was strewed with wounded
over whom it was hardly possible sometimes to avoid
moving. Wounded or mutilated horses wandered
or hurried in circles, — the noise was deafening & the
air of ruin & destruction that prevailed wherever
the eye could reach - gave nothing of the exhilaration of victory. Lord Uxbridge in Hussar uniform
mounted on a common Troop horse his own being exhausted
rode with General Vivian a short time in our front.
Colonel Sir Felton Harvey came to exchange his wounded
horse - & in the act of mounting a Troop horse of the 10th
exclaimed "Lord Wellington has won the Battle if
could but get the d——d   to advance."
then galloped to the front.

[left margin notes:]
Major Percy we
of the fall of Si[r]
..only, & of the
d of Col. Frederick
..onby.

..quietly we heard
..nd of Col. Hay 16th
..

..we joined for a
General Vandeleur's
..de.

18th June 1815 Moving down in open column of Squadrons the Regiments formed line & attached, Sir Hussey Vivian at the head.

On coming on a Chaussée – or road – a column of French Artillery moving across from our left were fallen in with – whilst on our right there was a cluster of French Cavalry – as they gave way their Officer moved forward to fire his pistol at the leader of the 18th. The Charge then ceased to be compact for the assailants & those who were in retreat were intermingled pellmell, & that as hard as they could ride.

[Officers who led squadrons of the 18th Hussars. • Major Grant. Cap[t]. Luard (his horse wounded) Cap[t] Croker / broke his sword in the charge: • L[t] Hesse wounded severely in the arm • L[t] & Adj[t] Duperier horse wounded & himself severely wounded in the head. • L[t] Machell horse killed in the charge. • L[t] Rowell horse wounded.]

There were many French Infantry, & some of the Ancienne Garde (calmly retiring in the tumult) here sabred, & Cuirassiers & other French Cavalry endeavouring to outride pursuit – In the way a Square or two of French Infantry were passed not coming exactly into the stream of attack of the 18th as they pressed on – the Squares were to our right – & were charged by the 10th Hussars in which Major Hon[ble] Frederick Howard was unfortunately killed.

The first discrimination of active pursuit which took place with the 18th was in a Hollow way.

Some Squares of French infantry were on the opposite bank & to that bank there was some intervening fence which rendered attack upon the nearly if not quite impracticable & at all events certain to fail. [Many other officers & parties of the 18th were as forward as this party, which is mentioned with L[t] Woodberry.]

At this particular time & place L[t] Woodberry happened to be remarked by the narrator with some of the 18th well formed up & perhaps also Lieut. Waldie was there. From the nature of such an attack as had taken place with as much animation & zeal the pursuit had unavoidably diverged in different directions, whence it was necessary to withdraw in order to formation. The 18th were then brought back, on the suggestion & palpable evidence, that nothing more could be done at the moment. – [There were a good many men with (...) in returning. The shot struck them as they galloped – & several men & Horses w[d] fall at once.] The Charge as also the previous movement had been attended with casualty – but retiring with a view to formation proved infinitely more destructive. – For as the light was uncertain they crossed upon some fire, whether the Enemy's or Prussians' (perhaps the latter) which mowed down many at a time more than once. – This was near a Farm House or some such building. – The 10th & 18th formed up together – & after a time were moved still farther to the right, & the action having concluded, Bivouacked. – For the attack the 1st Hussars had been in reserve. – In the course of the day the Brigade had moved from left to the right – & its charge was intermediate in direction between La Haie Sainte & Hugoumont. Sir Hussey Vivian severally addressed the Regiments that night in commendation of their conduct. [on returning with 18th met Sir Rob[t] Gardiner. Ld Rob[t] Manners was forming up 10th when 18th came up to them in which Maj[r] Grant assisted.]

moving down in open column of Squadrons the
Regiments formed line & attacked, Sir Hussey Vivian
at the head.

On coming on a Chaussée — or road — a column of French
artillery moving across from our left were fallen in
with — whilst on our right there was a cluster of
French Cavalry — as they gave way, their officer moved
forward to fire his pistol as the leader of the 10ᵗʰ. the
charge then ceased to be compact for the assailants
& those who were in retreat were intermingled
pellmell, & that as hard as they could ride.
There were many French Infantry, & some of
the ancienne Garde (calmly retiring in the turmoil) there
sabred, & Cuirassiers & other French Cavalry endeavouring to outride pursuit — In this way a Square
or two of French Infantry were passed not coming
exactly into the stream of attack of the 18ᵗʰ as they
passed on — the Squares were to our right — & were
charged by the 10ᵗʰ Hussars in which Major Honble
Frederick Howard was unfortunately killed.

The first diminution of active pursuit which took
place with the 18ᵗʰ was in a Hollow way.

Some Squares of French infantry were on the opposite bank & to their bank there was some intervening
fence which rendered attack upon them nearly if
not quite impracticable & at all events certain to
fail

At this particular time & place Lt. Woodberry happened
to be remarked by the narrator with some of the 18ᵗʰ
well formed up, & perhaps also Lieut. Waldie was there
from the nature of such an attack as had taken
place with so much animation & zeal the pursuit had
unavoidably diverged in different directions, whence
it was necessary to withdraw in order to formation.
The 18ᵗʰ were then brought back, on the suggestion &
palpable evidence, that nothing more could be done at
that moment. — The charge as also the previous
movement had been attended with casualty — but
retiring with a view to formation proved infinitely more destructive — for as the light was uncertain
they crossed upon some fire, whether the Enemy's or
Prussian's (perhaps the latter) which mowed down
many at a time more than once. — this was near
a farm House or some such building. — The 10ᵗʰ & 18ᵗʰ
formed up together — & after a time were moved still
farther to the right, & the action having concluded
Bivouacked. — In the attack the 1ˢᵗ Hussars had been
in reserve. — In the course of this day the Brigade had
moved from left to the right — & its charge was intermediate
in direction between La Haie Sainte & Hugomont
Sir Hussey Vivian severally addressed the Regiments
that night in commendation of their conduct

officers who led
Squadrons of the
18ᵗʰ Hussars.

Sir Grant

—— Duard (Hoke
wounded)

—— Croker (broke his
sword in the charge

—— Espe wounded
severely in the arm

& Lady. Duperier
were wounded
—— severely,
wounded in the head.

Machell horse
killed in the charge.

Rowlls horse
wounded.

—— & other officers
& ranks of the 18ᵗʰ were
forward as this
stage which is
mentioned with Lt.
Woodberry

we were a good
many men with them
returning.
—— they struck them
—— they Galloped —
—— several men
horses we fall
—— at once.

returned with 18ᵗʰ
& Sir Robt. Gardiner.
& Robt. Manners
as coming up 10ᵗʰ
when 18ᵗʰ came up to
them in which they
were assisted.

LIEUTENANT COLONEL SIR WILLIAM MAYNARD GOMM

19 JUNE 1815

Lieutenant-Colonel Sir William Maynard Gomm, Assistant Quartermaster-General, writes to his sister Sophia the day after the battle.

"I know what satisfaction it will give you all to learn that I have been wit the 5th Division, and therefore in the hottest of all this 'Glorious Business' and have escaped with two Blows which are of no Consequence, and two Horses wounded which is of great consequence –

The Prussians are marching upon Charleroy, and we move upon Nivelles immediately –

I consider the French army as utterly destroyed, and we shall be in Paris as fast as our legs can carry us – tell aunt so, and recommend her to leave off croaking –

I am writing this unintelligibly enough, but it would be still worse by word of mouth, at this moment, for I am so hoarse with hurraaing all yesterday, that I can scarcely articulate –

I have been four days without facing face or hands, but am in hourly expectation of my lavender water &c &c &c

I am very tired – adieu dear Sophia, I hope this will reach you early, for I will know how anxious you will all be about me –

…

We have done nothing like it since Blenheim and the Consequences are likely to be far more important …"

Camp of Waterloo
19th June 1815

My dear Sophia,

I know what satisfaction
it will give you all to learn,
that I have been with the 5th
Division, and therefore in the
hottest of all this glorious Barney
and have escaped with two
Blows which are of no Consequence, and two Horses wounded
which is of great consequence.

The Prussians are marching
upon Charleroy, and we move
upon Nivelles immediately,

I consider the French Army
as utterly destroyed, and we

shall be in Paris as fast
as our legs can carry us. —
Tell Aunt to tend Veronica
but to leave off croaking. —

I am writing this unintelli-
-gibly enough, but it would
be still worse by word of mouth,
at this moment, for I am so
hoarse with harangueing all
yesterday, that I can scarcely
articulate —

I have been four days without
washing face or hands, but
am in hourly expectation of
my Lavender Water &c. &c. —
I am very tired. Adieu
dear Sophia. I hope this will

reach you early, for I well
know how anxious you will
all be about me.

Best love to Aunt Henry
Foulke, and all friends.

I have not yet fallen in
with Humboldt, but must
shortly.

I shall direct my letter
to Foulke's, not knowing where
you are exactly.

I am much afraid
Mr Foulke will be called
upon to illuminate furiously
on this occasion — We have seen
nothing like it since Blucher
and the four geese are likely to be
far more important, ten times
once more. Ever your af-
fectionate brother Benjamin

THE END FOR NAPOLEON

IN LONDON, THE PRINCE REGENT was at a ball in St James's Square on the night of 21 June, when there was a great commotion in the street outside. One of Wellington's aides-de-camp, Major Henry Percy – still covered in the dust of battle – leapt from a coach, raced into the house and dropped on one knee before the Prince with the words, "Victory, Sire! Victory!"

The news was received with great jubilation all over the country. Church bells rang as the news arrived in village after village. Wellington's despatch was printed in full in *The Times* newspaper of 22 June: "Glory to Wellington, to our gallant soldiers and to our brave allies," trumpeted the paper. "Bonaparte's reputation has been wrecked."

Napoleon, riding with all speed for the French frontier, crossed the river Sambre at 5am on 19 June. He arrived at the Elysée Palace in Paris at 5.30 on 21 June, claiming that "panic had seized the army". He blamed Ney and Grouchy for the defeat, and still hoped to muster enough men to fight on. But the French parliament would have none of it and rejected Napoleon's call for further resistance. Within 24 hours of his return, the Emperor had abdicated in favour of his son, whom he referred to as Napoleon II. It was a desperate attempt to prolong the dynasty, but that too was rejected by the French parliament.

The ex-emperor now set his heart on finding sanctuary in the United States, which had been closely aligned with France for most of the previous four decades.

At the end of June, he travelled to the port of Rochefort on the Bay of Biscay coast. However, it soon became clear to him that he wouldn't evade the British navy's blockade, and on 15 July he handed himself over to the protection of the captain of a blockading British warship HMS *Bellerophon*. Napoleon wrote a letter to the Prince Regent in London appealing to him as "the most powerful, the most constant and the most generous of my enemies," and asked that he be allowed to throw himself on the "hospitality of the English people".

The British prime minister, Lord Liverpool, was horrified. His view was that Napoleon should have been tried and executed, preferably by the newly restored

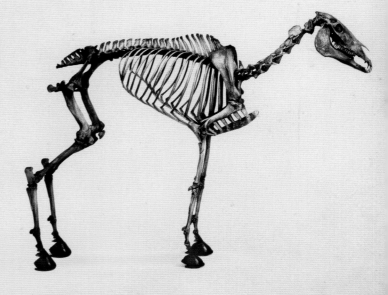

Below: Skeleton of Napoleon's horse Marengo, an Arab stallion with a light grey coat, standing just over 14 hands high. Napoleon named him after his victory at Marengo in 1800 and rode him at his later victories of Austerlitz, Jena and Wagram. After Napoleon's defeat at Waterloo, Marengo was kept at stud in Britain and died in 1831. The skeleton was preserved and passed to the Royal United Service Institute in London.

French government of Louis XVIII. But Wellington, now the undisputed commander-in-chief of all the allied armies moving in to occupy France, strongly opposed any move to execute his former antagonist. The most vocal threat had come from the Prussian commander, Marshal Blücher. He and his army had rampaged their way through to Paris, vandalising and looting French property on the way. He now demanded from Wellington that Napoleon be seized and handed over to the Prussian army for summary execution. He also insisted that the bridge over the Seine called the Pont d'Iéna – built by Napoleon to celebrate the French victory over Prussia in 1806 – be destroyed. Blücher saw the bridge as an insulting reminder of his country's

humiliation nine years earlier. Wellington rejected both requests.

Captain Frederick Maitland of the *Bellerophon* described his eminent new passenger as strong and well built, about 170 cm (5 feet, 7 inches) tall, with a "light sallow" complexion. He noted that he was "corpulent", and that while on board the ship he was lethargic and seemed to have lost much of his mental energy. Maitland anchored off the south coast of England while the government in London agonized about what to do with the man whose campaigns had cost millions of lives across Europe. All agreed that the ex-emperor should be "denied the means or opportunity of again disturbing the peace of Europe and renewing all the calamities of war".

Above: Napoleon leaves the battlefield of Waterloo on the evening of 18 June. He was across the border into France early the following morning and was in Paris two days later. He abdicated 24 hours afterwards when it became clear that the French parliament would not support any further resistance.

PERCY'S PURSE

After Wellington wrote his victory dispatch just hours after Napoleon's defeat, he handed it to one of his staff officers, Major Henry Percy, and ordered him to hurry to London and give it to the Secretary for War, Earl Bathurst. Percy folded the letter and put it in a scented, purple velvet purse that the handsome major had been given by an unnamed dancing partner at the Duchess of Richmond's ball. Wellington also gave Percy two captured French standards to place at the feet of the Prince Regent. When Percy was rushed to London in a four-horse coach three days later, he was described as "a dusty figure with a flag in each hand". He presented the flags to the Prince with the words "Victory, Sire! Victory!"

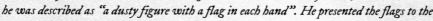

But how to deny him the means? All sorts of locations were bandied about for his incarceration from the Tower of London to Fort George in Scotland. In the end, the prevailing argument was that Napoleon should be exiled to a spot from which escape would be well nigh impossible, and a Whitehall civil servant suggested St Helena. It was a British territory, more than 1,600 km (1,000 miles) from anywhere in the middle of the South Atlantic Ocean. Lord Liverpool approved. Oddly, the Duke of Wellington played no part in the decision-making, although Napoleon chose to hold him responsible for it.

When HMS *Bellerophon* anchored a mile off Brixham in Torbay, word soon got around that she was carrying an exceptional cargo. An inquisitive passing boatman, craning to see who or what was on board the warship, was rewarded with a message thrown furtively to him in a bottle. "We have got Bonaparte on board!" The news was all around town within minutes, and sightseers soon gathered in thousands. Some cheered, probably to attract Napoleon's attention; most just stared. All watched in fascination as the ex-emperor repeatedly appeared at

the gangway lifting his hat and bowing to the crowd. But any hopes he had of being granted some kind of asylum in Britain were soon dashed when the ship was moved to Plymouth and he was told that he would be transferred to HMS *Northumberland* and taken to St Helena. His escort into exile was to be Rear Admiral Sir George Cockburn.

Cockburn was a fiery buccaneering seaman of Scottish descent who had the distinction of being the prime mover in the burning of Washington in August 1814. In the War of 1812 with the United States, he conducted a series of uncompromising raids on the American coast, and when the British government sent a task force to give the Americans what Whitehall described as a "a good drubbing", Cockburn persuaded its commander to throw caution to the wind and attack and burn the United States capital. He was one of the first to enter the White House, which had been abandoned by the president and his wife, who had conveniently left dinner on the table. The invaders, encouraged by Cocbkurn, promptly ate the meal and then set fire to the place. Eleven months later, with peace restored with the United States as well as

France, this formidable admiral was given the daunting task of accompanying the bitterly resentful French ex-emperor to his final lonely retreat.

"How do you do, General Bonaparte?" asked Cockburn. The admiral made it clear to the *Northumberland's* crew that he would not countenance the use of the word "emperor". Nor would he allow anyone to raise his hat to Napoleon. It wasn't long before Napoleon was describing Cockburn as "rough and overbearing". The admiral was nevertheless captivated by Napoleon's conversations at dinner in the ship's wardroom. On one occasion, Napoleon said that if he had won the battle of Waterloo, he would have contemplated a truce with Britain. Cockburn promptly replied that no British government would have trusted him to keep his word. A handful of the ex-emperor's own attendants were allowed to accompany him to St Helena, including the *Bellerophon's* Irish surgeon, Dr Barry O'Meara, whom Napoleon liked.

The voyage to St Helena took more than two months. On 15 October, the

Northumberland finally anchored in the harbour and Napoleon was taken ashore. It wasn't long before his staff were complaining that the "Emperor" was unhappy about his temporary lodgings. "I have no cognizance", wrote Cockburn pompously, "of any emperor being actually on this island." If Napoleon found Cockburn's supervision

Left: Gold watch with key owned by Napoleon, made by the expert Swiss watchmaker Abraham Louis Breguet, Paris. After his defeat at Waterloo and exile to St Helena, Napoleon presented the watch to the governor of the island, Sir Hudson Lowe.

Below: Napoleon on the deck of HMS *Bellerophon*. He despaired of escaping across the Atlantic to the United Sates and appealed to the Prince Regent in London for some kind of asylum in England. He was refused and shipped off to St Helena, a remote island in the South Atlantic.

GEORGE COCKBURN
1772–1853

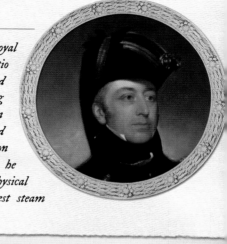

Audacious, energetic and ruthless, George Cockburn joined the Royal Navy aged nine as a captain's servant. A favourite of Horatio Nelson, he commanded ships during the French Revolutionary and Napoleonic wars. As well as infuriating Americans by burning the White House, Rear Admiral Cockburn blockaded American ports and ravaged towns during the War of 1812. He also freed nearly 2,000 slaves from Florida. After depositing Napoleon on St Helena, he became a British MP. As First Naval Lord, he founded a gunnery school at Portsmouth, discouraged physical punishment of sailors and made sure the navy had the latest steam and screw technology.

Above: A British cartoon (captioned *The Ex-Emperor in a Bottle*) shows the victorious allied commanders and heads of state presenting the defeated Napoleon to the restored French King Louis XVIII. From left to right: the Russian General Count Platov, whose Cossacks hounded Napoleon's army after his defeat at Leipzig in 1813; the Duke of Wellington; Marshal Blücher; General Schwarzenburg, the Austrian commander at Leipzig; the British Prince Regent, proudly holding a gun symbolizing the allied victory at Waterloo; Emperor Francis I of Austria; Czar Alexander I of Russia; King Frederick III of Prussia.

somewhat heavy-handed, he would find that of his successor, Sir Hudson Lowe, utterly intolerable. Lowe had to implement a whole set of petty restrictions ordered by the government which provoked Napoleon into making a string of complaints against him.

Napoleon survived six years on St Helena, recounting to Dr O'Meara and to his own French attendants his version of history. He blamed everyone but himself for his defeat at Waterloo, accusing Ney, Soult, d'Erlon and Grouchy of having effectively disobeyed his orders and lost him the battle. He had praised Wellington in the past, but on St Helena he went out of his way to belittle him. He admired the way the allied troops had fought but claimed Wellington's strategy at Waterloo was "deplorable" and that the position he'd taken up on the ridge of Mont St Jean was "completely impossible". He believed that Wellington had left himself no scope for retreat with dense woods behind him. He also believed, wrongly, that Wellington had urged his exile to St Helena.

Wellington was not so ungracious about Napoleon. Although he had his doubts about his opponent's personal tastes, he had none about his military professionalism. When asked whom he considered to be the greatest soldier of the age, Wellington replied, "In this age, in past ages, in any age, Napoleon."

Below: Napoleon dictates his memoirs - in which he criticized nearly everyone except himself - to Count Las Cases on the island of St Helena in 1816. He lived another five years in captivity on the island until his death in May 1821.

The Society of Painters of Oil and WATER COLOURS will CLOSE their ELEVENTH ANNUAL EXHIBITION on Saturday next, June 24th, at the Great Rooms, Spring Gardens.—Admission, 1s., Catalogue 6d.
C. V. FIELDING, Secretary.

Interior of Paris, Barker's Panorama, Strand, near Surrey Street. A VIEW of PARIS, taken from the Tuileries, comprising the Garden and Place Carrousel, the Quays, the Bridges, and most of the public buildings, with the hills commanding the City, which are now fortifying by Buonaparte, is open in the large circle.

British Gallery, Pall Mall. This GALLERY is now OPEN with a selection of Celebrated Pictures, by Rebecca Rembrandt Vandyke, and other eminent artists of the Flemish and Dutch Schools, with which the Proprietors have favoured the English institution for the gratification of the Nation, and for the benefit of the Fine Arts in general. Open from 9 till 6. Admittance, 1s; Catalogues, 1s.

On Sunday Morning next, a Sermon will be preached at St. Paul's, Covent Garden, for the benefit of the Charity Schools, belonging to that parish, by the Rev. GEORGE GASKIN, D.D., Rector of St. Benet, Grace Church, London, and of Stoke Newington, Middlesex. Prayers will begin at 11 o'clock.

St. Bride's, Fleet Street. A Sermon will be Preached in the above Church on Sunday next, June 25, for the BENEFIT of the CHARITY CHILDREN, belonging to the said parish, by the Rev. S. CROWTHER, A.M., Vicar of Christ Church, and Joint Lecturer of St. Botolph, Bishopsgate. Divine Service to begin at Eleven in the Morning. A Hymn will be sung by the children.

Society of Ireland. To-morrow, the 23rd of June, 1815, will be held at the New London Tavern, Cheapside, the ANNUAL MEETING of the BAPTIST SOCIETY for PROMOTING the GOSPEL in IRELAND. Breakfast at 7 o'clock, the Chair is to be taken at 8 precisely. The principal objects of this Institution are to establish schools in Ireland for teaching the native Irish language, and to employ persons to read the Holy Scriptures in Irish to their neighbours.

Spring Garden Novelty. At the Royal Exhibition Rooms, W. DE LA ROCHE, Mechanician, from Paris, will exhibit every morning and evening his Musical Automaton. First part, two beautiful Automata Figures, that will perform on the violin and tambourine. Second, a Mechanical Canary Bird, which sings ten different airs. Third, a Dutch Coffee-house vending all kinds of Figures by a mechanical process. Fourth, the Mysterious Column that will astonish every beholder. Fifth, a variety of Automata Figures which answer different questions. The public are respectfully informed that the above Automatous perform at the will of any person present. Admission in the day, 6s., in the evening at 8 o'clock, 2s.

Notice to Creditors. The Creditors of Charles Edmund Bull, deceased, of the late Finsbury Repository, White Street, Little Moorfields, are requested to meet the Administrators to his EFFECTS, at the White Bear, Basinghall Street, on Friday, the 30th inst., at 12 o'clock precisely, when a statement will be laid before them. June 17, 1815.

All Persons having any Claim or Demands on the ESTATE of MR. JAMES TURPIN, late of Pump Row, Old Street, in the parish of St. Luke's, in the county of Middlesex, Turner and Toyman, deceased, are requested to send an account and particulars thereof to Mr. William Dimes, 18, Friday Street, Cheapside, Solicitor to the Administrator, and all persons who may be indebted to the Estate of the said James Turpin, are desired to pay the same without further notice.

Pursuant to a Decree of the High COURT of CHANCERY, made in a cause Anderson against Anderson, the Creditors of ANDALUSIA HASLAM, late of Pershore, in the county of Worcester, Widow, deceased, are on or before the 18th day of July next, to come in and prove their debts before John Springett Harvey, Esq., one of the Masters of the said Court, at his Chambers in Southampton Buildings, Chancery Lane, London, or in default thereof, they will be peremptorily excluded the benefit of the said decease.

Pursuant to a Decree of the High COURT of CHANCERY, made in a cause Norton against Newman, all persons with whom John Harkness (who resided at Lisbon in Portugal, from about February, 1810, until March, 1811, when he died there) contracted any Debts during his residence in Portugal, between the time when the said John Harkness, at the time of his death, and are now owing, are forthwith to come in and prove their several debts before Francis Paul Stratford, Esq., one of the Masters of the said Court, at his Chambers in South-ampton Buildings, Chancery Lane, London, or in default thereof they will be excluded the benefit of the said decease.

Board and Lodging.—A Respectable private family residing in the neighbourhood of Brunswick Square, wish to receive one or two gentlemen as INMATES.—Cards of address at Mr. Spencer's Circulating Library, 22, Great Ormond Street.

Education.—Winton, near Borough, in Westmoreland.—BOYS are EDUCATED, furnished with books, boarded, and clothed by the Rev. J. Adamthwaite, D.D., beneficed Curate of Badly, at 22 guineas a year, and Parlour Boarders at 48 guineas. There are no vocations at this school, and from the close attention of Dr. A. and his assistants to the education of his scholars, no school in the kingdom can boast of finer boys. Dr. A., who was for many years an usher in the public schools, and tutor to a nobleman's family, attends each day between the hours of 11 and 1 at the Clapham Coffee House, St. Paul's. References to bishops, clergymen, and laymen of equal eminence.

A Respectable Youth is Wanted as an APPRENTICE to a Working Jeweller and Goldsmith.—Apply at 14, Charter House-street, Charter House-square. A premium is expected.

A Respectable Young Person Wants a SITUATION as BARMAID. She has lived in that capacity nine years, and can have an undeniable character from her employers.—Address to "S. W.," at Mr. Wood's, bricklayer, East-lane, Kent-road.

As Governess.—A Lady wishes to engage either as COMPANION or GOVERNESS in a Private Family. Respectable references will be given.—Direct to "G." at Mr. Birdsay's, grocer, 41, Goodge-street, Fitzroy-square.

To Dress Makers.—The Advertiser wishes to ENGAGE a PARTNER in a respectable concern in or near the City.—Apply or address, post paid, to "M. M.," at Mrs. Vidal's, 33, King-street, Holborn.

To Cabinet Makers.—A Young Man aged 20, wishes to ARTICLE himself to a respectable man for three years, to complete himself in the art of Cabinet Making.—Apply or address, post paid, to "G. E.," at the "Coopers," corner of Wood-street, Brown-lane, Brick-lane.

A Middle-aged Man Wants a Situation as UPPER SERVANT, in or out of Livery, or in a small family where there is but one kept. He can have an undeniable reference from the situation he has just left.—Direct, at "J. K.," 29, Riding House-lane.

A Lady, qualified by accomplishments and education, wishes for a SITUATION as GOVERNESS. She will undertake to teach History, Geography, Arithmetic, French, and the rudiments of Latin.—Address, post-paid, to "E. B.," at Mr. Hatchard's, Piccadilly.

Partnership.—Wanted, in an established CONCERN of the first respectability in the City (in consequence of the death of the late Partner), a person who can take an active part, and can command at least £13,000.—Apply, by letter, to "B. M.," at the Jerusalem Coffee House, Cooper's-court, Cornhill. None but principles or their agents will be attended to.

To Coach Makers.—Wanted, a SITUATION as JUNIOR CLERK in a Coach Maker's Counting-house, by a Young Man of respectable connexions, about the age of 22, who has been brought up in the business, and can give the most respectable references.—Address to "J. H.," 22, Cross-street, Hatton-garden.

A Lady on the point of quitting a Family where she has resided as Governess some time, wishes to engage in a similar SITUATION. Will undertake to teach the English and French languages grammatically and fluently, History, Geography, and the use of the Globes; the rudiments of Music, Writing, and Arithmetic.—Address, post paid, to "A. T. C.," 67, Cross-street, St. James's.

Cottage.—Wanted, between 20 and 30 Miles from Town, a small HOUSE at a moderate rent.—Address to "T. T.," 1, Chads-row, Gray's-inn-road.

House to be Sold by Private Contract.—A very eligible, genteel, and substantial HOUSE, with a handsome flower garden, secured at the end by a capital Coach House and Stable recently built on an approved plan by the present proprietor, pleasantly situated in the best part of Sloane Street, in a high state of repair, for the unexpired term of near 50 years, subject to the low ground rent of £17 17s. per annum. May be viewed between the hours of 12 and 4 by ticket only, to be had of Mr. Lorrimore, silk dyer, 340, Strand.

Gower Street, Bedford Square, east side to be SOLD the LEASE of a HOUSE in perfect repair, with long garden. The furniture may be taken at a valuation; also a Pew to be Let in the best part of Woburn Chapel.—Apply to Mr. Russell, upholsterer, Chancery-lane.

A French Gentleman, Partner in a most Respectable Mercantile House in the City, is desirous to BOARD and LODGE in a genteel family whose society would enable him to improve in the English language. He would prefer the vicinity of Russell Square, but has no objection to any other pleasant and airy situation out of the City.—Apply, by letter, "Z. Y.," to Mr. Charles, at Cazzaway's Coffee-house.

Guildhall, London, June 4, 1815.—The COMMITTEE of the CORPORATION of LONDON, appointed to carry into execution the Act of Parliament lately passed for building a new Prison within the City of London, will meet in the COUNCIL CHAMBER, Guildhall London, on WEDNESDAY, the 28th day of June, at ONE o'Clock in the afternoon precisely, to receive Proposals in writing sealed up, for the purchase of BONDS under the seal of the Corporation of London, of £1000 each, bearing an interest at £5 per Cent. per annum, to commence the 5th day of January last, and issued under the authority of the said Act.
(Signed)
WOODTHORPE.

Guildhall, London, June 16, 1815.—The Committee for letting the Bridge House Estate will meet at Guildhall, on THURSDAY, the 29th day of June instant, at TWO o'clock precisely, by PUBLIC AUCTION, to LET upon Building Leases, several LOTS of PIECES of GROUND, situate respectfully at the corner of Cresent Place, adjoining the entrance of the Indigent Blind School in Temple Place and Warwick Row, Blackfriars Road, in a new street or road leading from the Borough Road to Union Street, and Higlor's Lane on the east side of Union Street aforesaid, and on the south side of the Lambeth Roads.
Plans elevations, conditions, for letting the same may be seen at the Office of Works, Guildhall, London. (Signed)
SAMUEL NEWMAN, Comptroller.

A Lady engaged in a School for YOUNG LADIES, residing at the Sea at a distance of 70 miles from London, will be in Town till Thursday next, and any Families who may wish to take the advantage of her return to send the CHILDREN for the BENEFIT of SEA AIR or BATHING, or for INSTRUCTION, will have an opportunity by a line with the address to "A. B.," Holding's Hotel, Hanover Square. A French Teacher is wanted in the same establishment. Parlour Boarders received on moderate terms.

Furnished Apartments for Single GENTLEMEN, consisting of Sitting Room and Two Rooms, in a pleasant airy situation in the vicinity of Pentonville, where the are no children or other lodgers. The most respectable reference will be given and required.—Apply at 26, Great Sutton Street.

Board and Lodging in a Genteel PRIVATE FAMILY, where only two are taken. The society will be found cheerful and agreeable; the rooms are large and handsomely furnished. It is a pleasant airy situation, near Russell Square, Bloomsbury Square.—Apply to Mr. Porter, Baker, Constitution Row, Gray's-Inn-Road.

Counting House and Lodging.—A GENTLEMAN of RESPECTABILITY and Regular Habits may be accommodated with BREAKFAST and LODGING in a respectable quiet house, about five minute's walk from the Royal Exchange. A very commodious Counting House to be Let.—Enquire at 1, New Street, Crutchedfriars.

Furnished Country Lodgings.—A WIDOW of RESPECTABILITY will be happy to ACCOMMODATE a Small Family or Two Single Gentlemen with the chief part of her house, consisting of Three Bed Rooms and a Sitting Room, either together or separate. They are most pleasantly situated at Camberwell, have a good Garden, and detached Washhouse; a servant may be dispensed with; attendance undertaken. Terms moderate.—Address left at Mr. Savage, Baker, near the Gray's-Inn.

To Writing Masters.—Wanted, at an ACADEMY where the most liberal Salary is given, an able WRITING MASTER.—Direct, with Specimens, to "A. B.," 72, St. Paul's Church-yard.

Green Street, Grosvenor Square.—To be SOLD, with or without furniture, the unexpired LEASE of 7 years of a very convenient TWO-ROOMED HOUSE, situate in a preferable part of Green Street, and within sight of Hyde Park.—Apply, to Gillam and Co., 176, Oxford Street.

Education.—Wanted, for a Young GENTLEMAN, a SCHOOL in a healthy dry situation where there are a limited number of pupils not exceeding twelve, that considerable attention may be paid to his education.—Address, post paid, to "O. K.," 112, Goswell Street.

Preparatory School, Ramsgate.—Mrs. TRIST, of St. George's House, RECEIVES YOUNG GENTLEMEN for INSTRUCTION between the age of three and eight. The terms are moderate. A Lady is in town for a week who would undertake the care of any Young Gentleman intended for the establishment.—Address, at Mr. Larning's, 80, Ludgate Hill.

A Single Gentleman wishing to domesticate in a Genteel Private Family for the sake of agreeable society, can be accommodated with BOARD and LODGING on a very superior plan to what is usually offered. The house is well situated, within half a mile of the parks, and it is presumed would be found a very desirable acquisition to any gentleman whose avocations require his daily attendance in town.—Apply to "A. B.," at Mr. Eber's Library, Old Bond Street.

Worthing.—Board and Lodging.—BLOSS'S, from Milsom Street, Bath, have the honor to inform their friends and the visitors of Worthing that BEDFORD HOUSE is OPEN as usual for the Season, where they hope, from the well-known respectability of the establishment, and their united efforts to accommodate their friends, to be honored with a continuance of that favor they have so many years experienced.—Bedford House Worthing, June 15, 1815.

Family Hotel and Boarding House on the Beach, Exmouth, commanding views not surpassed in the kingdom of picturesque scenery, embracing a noble expanse of ocean, the River Exe, with its celebrated beautiful banks studded with gentlemen's seats, the City of Exeter and surrounding rich and cultivated county. R. MARK respectfully acquaints the Ladies and Gentlemen frequenting the Devonshire Coast that he has fitted up and furnished an establishment of the above description, which has long been a desideratum at that place. He trusts by unremitting assiduity to merit public support and patronage.

One Thousand Pounds will be presented to any person who can procure for a Gentleman of respectability an adequate MERCANTILE SITUATION.—Address, post paid, to "A. B.," 169, Swallow-street.

Pedal Harp and Cabinet Pianoforte, the property of a Clergyman. The Harp has had the Pedals green covered, &c., in complete order. Cost 45 guineas. To be Sold for 25 guineas. The Cabinet Pianoforte is as good as new, stands remarkably well, in tune, full in tone, two pedals, &c., for 38 guineas; shop price, 60 guineas. Square Pianoforte, 16 guineas. No abatement.—To be seen at 5, Leicester-place.

Music Taught.—A Young Lady of respectability, fully competent to teach the Pianoforte, whose time is not completely occupied, is desirous of ENGAGING with a few more Pupils, whom she would INSTRUCT on the above instrument on reasonable terms, or would have no objection to undertake the musical department in a School. She trusts her method will be found particularly adapted to facilitate improvements, having received her own instruction from eminent in the profession, to whom reference can be given if required.—Address, post paid, "E. G.," at Tinkler's Toy-rooms, 56, Bishopsgate-street, Within.

Snuff-box Makers Wanted.—Two or Three first-rate HANDS, as SNUFF-BOX MAKERS, in Gold and Silver.—Apply, to Hockley and Bosworth, Brook Street, Holborn.

Education.—Ladies' School and PRIVATE FAMILIES ATTENDED by a GENTLEMAN of professional and literary talents, who gives lessons in Writing, Arithmetic, Geography, Astronomy, Composition, Elocution, Criticism, and History. Respectable references.—Address, "M. A.," at Mr. Mather's, 20, Sun-street, Bishopsgate.

We have seen a gentleman who left Brussels on Sunday evening, at which time the people were manifesting the greatest joy for a decisive victory gained by the Duke of WELLINGTON on that day. The wounded were beginning to be brought in, in waggons, as that gentleman quitted Brussels.

Many of the British Officers present in the affirs of the 16th declared that they never witnessed more severe fighting in the Peninsula than that which took place on the plains of Fleurus and its vicinity. What made the fate of the 79th and 42d regiments so severe was their having been taken by surprise by a strong force of cuirassiers who lay in ambush for them in a road, the whole of which was completely intercepted by fields of corn immensely high. With such fury was the 79th Regiment attacked, that most of them were cut to pieces, and the whole were in danger of being destroyed but for the coming up of the brave 42d. This latter regiment formed itself into a square and five times were they broken. On the sixth attack they formed the plan of opening a passage to the enemy; and the moment he effected it, they changed their position, and so hemmed in the cuirassieurs, that not a single man was suffered to escape; thus was the destruction of one of BUONAPARTES finest regiments completed. Col. CAMERON says our informant was killed at the head of the gallant 42d. Next day Saturday, when the 79th was mustered, the men amounted to no more than 54 and two officers. A few more were, however expected to be brought in. General PICTON's division did wonders and the gallant General himself fought at the head of it in a manner to astonish the greatest veterans. The Duke of WELLINGTON exposed himself as usual to imminent danger; the bullets, says our informant, were whizzing about him in all directions.

Among other important proceedings, an Order in Council for reprisals and letters of marque against the French was agreed upon.

Thursday Morning 11 o'clk

We again stop the press to insert a copy of the *LONDON GAZETTE EXTRAORDINARY.*

THURSDAY, June 22, 1815.

DOWNING STREET, June 22.

Major the Honourable H. Percy arrived late last night with a dispatch from Field Marshal the Duke of WELLINGTON, K.G. to Earl BATHURST, his Majesty's Principal Secretary of State for the War Department, of which the following is a copy;—

Waterloo, June 19th 1815.

MY LORD,—Buonaparte having collected the 1st, 2d, 3rd, 4th, and 6th corps of the French army and the Imperial Guard, and nearly all the cavalry on the Sambre, and between that river and the Meuse, between the 10th and 14th of the month, advanced on the 15th and attacked the Prussian posts at Thuin and Lubez, on the Sambre, at daylight in the morning.

I did not hear of these events till the evening of the 15th, and immediately ordered the troops to prepare to march, and afterwards to march to their left, as soon as I had intelligence from other quarters to prove that the enemy's movements upon Charleroy was the real attack.

The enemy drove the Prussian posts from the Sambre on that day, and General Zieten who commanded the corps at Charleroy, retired upon Fleurus; and Marshal Prince Blucher concentrated the Prussian army upon Sambref holding the villages in front of his position of St. Amand and Ligny.

The enemy continued his march along the roadfromCharleroy towards Bruxelles, and on the same evening, the 15th attacked a brigade of the army of the Netherlands, under the Prince of Weimar, posted at Frasne, and forced it back to the farm house on the same road, called Les Quatre Bras.

The Prince of Orange immediately reinforced this brigade with another of the same division, under General Perponcher, and in the morning early regained part of the ground which had been lost, so as to have the command of the communications leading from Nivelles and Bruxelles, with Marshal Blucher's position.

In the mean time I had directed the whole army to march upon Les Quatre Bras, and the 5th division under Lieut. General Sir Thomas Picton, arrived at about half past two in the day, followed by the corps of troops under the Duke of Brunswick and afterwards by the contingent of Nassau.

At this time the enemy commenced an attack upon Prince Blucher with his whole force, excepting the 1st and 2d corps, and a corps of cavalry under General Kellerman, with which he attacked our posts at Les Quatre Bras.

The Prussian army maintained their position with their usual gallantry and perseverance, against a great disparity of number, as the 4th corps of their army, under General Bulow, had not joined, and I was not able to assist them as I wished, as I was attacked myself; and the troops, the cavalry in particular, which had a long distance to march, had not arrived.

We maintained our position also, and completely defeated and repulsed all the enemy's attempts to get possession of it. The enemy repeatedly attacked us with a large body of cavalry and infantry supported by a numerous and powerful artillery; he made several charges with the cavalry upon our infantry, but all were repulsed in the steadiest manner.

In this affair His Royal Highness the Prince of Orange the Duke of Brunswick, and Lieutenant Sir Thomas Picton, and Major General Sir James Kempt, and Sir Denis Pack, who were engaged from the commencement of the enemy's attack, highly distinguished themselves, as well as Lieutenant General Charles Baron Alten, Major General Sir C. Halket, Lieutenant General Cooke, and Major Generals Maitland and Byng, as they successively arrived. The troops of the 5th division and those of the Brunswick corps were long and severely engaged and conducted themselves with the utmost gallantry. I must particularly mention the 28th, the 42d, 79th, and 92d regiments and the battalion of Hanoverians.

Our loss was great, as your Lordship will perceive by the enclosed return, and I have particularly to regret his Serene Highness the Duke of Brunswick, who fell, fighting gallantly at the head of his troops.

Although Marshal Blucher had maintained his position at Sambref, he still found himself much weakened by the severity of the contest, in which he had been engaged, and as the 4th, corps had not arrived, he determined to fall back and concentrate his army upon Wavre; and he marched in the night after the action was over.

This movement of the Marshal rendered necessary a corresponding one on my part; and I retired from the farm of Quatre Bras upon Genappe, and thence upon Waterloo the next morning, the 17th, at ten o'clock.

The enemy made no effort to pursue Marshal Blucher. On the contrary, a patrole which I sent to Sambref in the morning, found all quiet, as the enemy's videttes fell back as the patrole advanced. Neither did he attempt to molest our march to the rear, although made in the middle of the day, excepting by following, with a large body of cavalry brought from his right, the Earl of Uxbridge.

This gave Lord Uxbridge an opportunity of charging them with the 1st Life Guards upon their debouche from the village of Genappe, upon which occasion his Lordship has declared himself to be well satisfied with that regiment.

The position which I took up in front of Waterloo, crossed the high roads from Charleroy and Nivelle, and had its right thrown back to a ravine near Merke Braine, which was occupied and its left extended to a height above the hamlet Ter la Haye, which was likewise occupied. In front of the right centre and near the Nivelle road, we occupied the house and garden of Hougoumont, which covered the return of that flank and in the front of the left centre, we occupied the farm of La Haye Sainte.

By our left we communicated with Marshal Prince Blucher at Wavre, through Ohaim; and the Marshal had promised me, that in case we should be attacked, he would support me with one or more corps, as might be necessary

The enemy collected his army, with the exception of the third corps, which had been sent to observe Marshal Blucher on a range of heights in our front, in the course of the night of the 17th and yesterday morning; and at about ten o'clock he commenced a furious attack upon our posts at Hougoumont, I had occupied that post with a detachment from General Byng's brigade of Guards, which was in position in its rear; and it was for some time under the command of Lieutenant Colonel Macdonel; and afterwards of Colonel Home; and I am happy to add, that it was maintained throughout the day with the utmost gallantry by these brave troops, notwithstanding the repeated efforts of large bodies of the enemy to obtain possession of it.

The attack upon the right of our centre was accompanied by a very heavy cannonade upon our whole line which was destined to support the repeated attacks of cavalry and infantry occasionally mixed, but sometimes separate, which were made upon it. In one of these the enemy carried the farm house of La Haye Sainte as the detachment of the light battalion of the legion which occupied it had expended all its ammunition, and the enemy occupied the only communication there was with them.

The enemy repeatedly charged our infantry with his cavalry but these attacks were uniformly unsuccessful and they afforded opportunities to our cavalry to charge, in one of which Lord E. Somerset's brigade, consisting of the life guards, royal horse guards, and first dragoon guards, highly distinguished themselves as did that of Major General Sir W. Ponsonby, having taken many prisoners and an eagle.

These attacks were repeated till about seven in the evening when the enemy made a desperate effort with the cavalry and infantry, supported by the fire of artillery, to force our left centre near the farm of La Haye Sainte, which after a severe contest was defeated, and having observed that the troops retired from this attack in great confusion, and that the march of General Bulew's corps by Euschermont upon Planchenorte and La Belle alliance, had begun to take effect and as I could perceive the fire of his cannon and as Marshal Prince Blucher had joined in person, with a corps of his army to the left of our line by Ohaim, I determined to attack the enemy, and immediately advanced the whole line of infantry, supported by the cavalry and artillery. The attack succeeded in every point; the enemy was forced from his position on the heights, and fled in the utmost confusion, leaving behind him as far as I could judge, one hundred and fifty pieces of cannon, with their ammunition, which fell into our hands. I continued the pursuit till long after dark, and then discontinued it only on account of the fatigue of our troops, who had been engaged during twelve hours, and because I found myself on the same road with Marshal Blucher, who assured me of his intention to follow the enemy throughout the night; he has sent me word this morning that he has taken sixty pieces of cannon belonging to the Imperial Guard, and several carriages, baggage &c. belonging to Buonaparte, in Genappe.

I propose to move, this morning, upon Nivelles, and not to discontinue my operations.

Your Lordship will observe, that such a desperate action could not be fought, and such advantages could not be gained, without great loss; and I am sorry to add, that ours has been immense. In Lieutenant General Sir Thomas Picton, his Majesty has sustained the loss of an officer who has frequently distinguished himself in his service, and he fell, gloriously leading his division to a charge of bayonets, by which one of the most serious attacks made by the enemy on our position, was defeated. The Earl of Uxbridge, after having successfully got through this arduous day, received a wound by almost the last shot fired, which will, I am afraid, deprive his Majesty for some time of his services.

His Royal Highness the Prince of Orange distinguished himself by his gallantry and conduct till he received a wound from a musket ball through the shoulder which obliged him to quit the field.

It gives me the greatest satisfaction to assure your Lordship, that the army never, upon any occasion, conducted itself better. The division of guards, under Lieutenant General Cooke, who is severely wounded; Major General Maitland and Major General Byng, set an example which was followed by all; and there is no Officer nor description of troops that did not behave well.

I must however particularly mention to his Royal Highnesses approbation Lieutenant General Sir H. Clinton, Major General Adam, Lieutenant General Charles Baron Alten, severely wounded, Major General Sir Colin Halbet, severely wounded; Colonel Ompteda, commanding a brigade of the 4th division; Major General Sir James Kemp, and Sir Denis Pack, Major General Lambert, Major General Lord E. Somerset; Major General Sir W. Ponsonby; Major General Sir C. Grant, and Major General Sir H. Vivian, Major General Sir O. Vandeleur; Major General Count Dornberg. I am also particularly indebted to General Lord Hill for assistance and conduct upon this as upon all former occasions.

The Artillery and Engineer departments were conducted much to my satisfaction by Colonel Sir G. Wood and Col. Smyth; and I had every reason to be satisfied with the conduct of the Adjt. General Major Gen. Barnes, who was wounded, and of the Quarter Master General Col. Delancy who was killed by a cannon shot in the middle of the action. This officer is a serious loss to his Majesty's Service and to me at this moment. I was likewise much indebted to the assistance of Lieutenant Colonel Lord Fitzroy Somerset, who was severely wounded, and of the officers composing my personal staff, who have suffered severely in this action. Lieutenant Colonel the Honourable Sir Alexander Gordon who was killed of his wounds was a most promising officer and is a serious loss to his Majesty's Service.

General Kruse, of the Nassau service, likewise conducted himself to my satisfaction, as did General Trip, commanding the heavy brigade of cavalry, and General Vanhope, commanding a brigade of infantry of the King of the Netherlands.

General Pozzi di Borgo, General Baron Vincent, General Muffling, and General Alvoa, were in the field during the action, and rendered me every assistance in their power. Baron Vincent is wounded, but I hope not severely; and General Pozzi di Borgo received a contusion

I should not do justice to my feelings or to Marshal Blucher and the Prussian army, if I did not attribute the successful result of this arduous day, to the cordial and timely assistance I received from them.

The operation of General Bulow, upon the enemy's flank, was a most decisive one; and even if I had not found myself in a situation to make the attack, which produced the final result, it would have forced the enemy to retire if his attacks should have failed, and would have prevented him from taking advantage of them if they should unfortunately have succeeded.

I send, with this despatch, two eagles, taken by the troops in this action, which Major Percy will have the honour of laying at the feet of his Royal Highness.

I beg leave to recommend him to your Lordship's protection. I have the honour, &c., (Signed,)

WELLINGTON.

P.S. Since writing the above, I have received a report that Major General Sir William Ponsonby is killed, and, in announcing this intelligence to your Lordship, I have to add the expression of my grief for the fate of an officer who had already rendered very brilliant and important services, and was an ornament to his profession.

2d P. S. I have not yet got the returns of killed and wounded, but I enclose a list of officers killed and wounded on the two days, as far as the same can be made out without the returns; and I am very happy to add, that Colonel de Lancey is not dead, and that strong hopes of his recovery are entertained.

[Here follows a list of the killed and wounded, which is the same as that appended to the letter to the Lord Mayor in our next page.]

PRIVATE CORRESPONDENCE.

Hamburg June 13,

Yesterday our first contingent of troops, consisting of a battalion of infantry and a squadron of cavalry, set out for the Netherlands, to join the army under the Duke of Wellington,

The Lubec contingent, destined also for the army of Wellington arrived to-day at Hamburg, where it was received with Hanseatic fraternity.

The following letter from Bremen of the 8th instant communicates further information as to the march of the Hanseatic troops.

"On the 14th instant, our contingent will break up from hence for the army. On the 15th the first division of the Hamburghers will enter, on the 18th the Lubeckers and on the 19th the second division of the Hamburg contingent. Their route is by Wildeshausen Linum,&c., for Antwerp."

Field Marshal Barclay de Tolly, with some thousands of Russian troops, attended the funeral of Marshal Berthier at Hamburg.

The public are anxious here lest too much time be given the common enemy.

THE TIMES

22 JUNE 1815

The Times, 22 June 1815, containing a full transcript of the Duke of Wellington's 19 June Waterloo dispatch. It is addressed to Earl Bathurst, a good friend of Wellington's and then Secretary of State for War and the Colonies.

To Earl Bathurst.

Waterloo, 19th June 1815.

MY LORD—Buonaparte, having collected the 1st, 2nd, 3rd, 4th, and 6th corps of the French army, and the Imperial Guards, and nearly all the cavalry, on the Sambre, and between that river and the Meuse, between the 10th and 14th of the month, advanced on the 15th and attacked the Prussian posts at Thuin and Lobbes, on the Sambre, at day-light in the morning.

I did not hear of these events till in the evening of the 15th; and I immediately ordered the troops to prepare to march, and, afterwards to march to their left, as soon as I had intelligence from other quarters to prove that the enemy's movement upon Charleroi was the real attack.

The enemy drove the Prussian posts from the Sambre on that day; and General Ziethen, who commanded the corps which had been at Charleroi, retired upon Fleurus; and Marshal Prince Blücher concentrated the Prussian army upon Sombref, holding the villages in front of his position of St. Amand and Ligny.

The enemy continued his march along the road from Charleroi towards Bruxelles; and, on the same evening, the 15th, attacked a brigade of the army of the Netherlands, under the Prince de Weimar, posted at Frasne, and forced it back to the farm house, on the same road, called Les Quatre Bras.

The Prince of Orange immediately reinforced this brigade with another of the same division, under General Perponcher,

and, in the morning early, regained part of the ground which had been lost, so as to have the command of the communication leading from Nivelles and Bruxelles with Marshal Blücher's position.

In the mean time, I had directed the whole army to march upon Les Quatre Bras; and the 5th division, under Lieutenant General Sir Thomas Picton, arrived at about half past two in the day, followed by the corps of troops under the Duke of Brunswick, and afterwards by the contingent of Nassau.

At this time the enemy commenced an attack upon Prince Blücher with his whole force, excepting the 1st and 2nd corps, and a corps of cavalry under General Kellermann, with which he attacked our post at Les Quatre Bras.

The Prussian army maintained their position with their usual gallantry and perseverance against a great disparity of numbers, as the 4th corps of their army, under General Bülow, had not joined; and I was not able to assist them as I wished, as I was attacked myself, and the troops, the cavalry in particular, which had a long distance to march, had not arrived.

We maintained our position also, and completely defeated and repulsed all the enemy's attempts to get possession of it. The enemy repeatedly attacked us with a large body of infantry and cavalry, supported by a numerous and powerful artillery. He made several charges with the cavalry upon our infantry, but all were repulsed in the steadiest manner.

In this affair, His Royal Highness the Prince of Orange, the Duke of Brunswick, and Lieutenant General Sir Thomas Picton, and Major Generals Sir James Kempt and Sir Denis Pack, who were engaged from the commencement of the enemy's attack, highly distinguished themselves, as well as Lieutenant General Charles Baron Alten, Major General Sir C. Halkett, Lieutenant

General Cooke, and Major Generals Maitland and Byng, as they successively arrived. The troops of the 5th division, and those of the Brunswick corps, were long and severely engaged, and conducted themselves with the utmost gallantry. I must particularly mention the 28th, 42nd, 79th, and 92nd regiments, and the battalion of Hanoverians.

Our loss was great, as your Lordship will perceive by the enclosed return; and I have particularly to regret His Serene Highness the Duke of Brunswick, who fell fighting gallantly at the head of his troops.

Although Marshal Blücher had maintained his position at Sombref, he still found himself much weakened by the severity of the contest in which he had been engaged, and, as the 4th corps had not arrived, he determined to fall back and to concentrate his army upon Wavre; and he marched ill the night, after the action was over.

This movement of the Marshal rendered necessary a corresponding one upon my part; and I retired from the farm of Quatre Bras upon Genappe, and thence upon Waterloo, the next morning, the 17th, at ten o'clock.

The enemy made no effort to pursue Marshal Blücher. On the contrary, a patrole which I sent to Sombref in the morning found all quiet*; and the enemy's vedettes fell back as the patrole advanced. Neither did he attempt to molest our march to the rear, although made in the middle of the day, excepting by following, with a large body of cavalry brought from his right, the cavalry under the Earl of Uxbridge.

This gave Lord Uxbridge an opportunity of charging them with the 1st Life Guards, upon their debouche from the village of Genappe, upon which occasion his Lordship has declared himself to be well satisfied with that regiment.

The position which I took up in front of Waterloo crossed the high roads from Charleroi and Nivelles, and had its right thrown back to a ravine near Merke Braine, which was occupied, and its left extended to a height above the hamlet Ter la Haye, which was likewise occupied. In front of the right centre, and near the Nivelles road, we occupied the house and gardens of Hougoumont, which covered the return of that flank; and in front of the left centre we occupied the farm of La Haye Sainte. By our left we communicated with Marshal Prince Blücher at Wavre, through Ohain; and the Marshal had promised me that, in case we should be attacked, he would support me with one or more corps, as might be necessary.

The enemy collected his army, with the exception of the 3rd corps, which had been sent to observe Marshal Blücher, on a range of heights in our front, in the course of the night of the 17th and yesterday morning, and at about ten o'clock he commenced a furious attack upon our post at Hougoumont. I had occupied that post with a detachment from General Byng's brigade of Guards, which was in position in its rear; and it was for some time under the command of Lieutenant Colonel Macdonell, and afterwards of Colonel Home; and I am happy to add that it was maintained throughout the day with the utmost gallantry by these brave troops, notwithstanding the repeated efforts of large bodies of the enemy to obtain possession of it.

This attack upon the right of our centre was accompanied by a very heavy cannonade upon our whole line, which was destined to support the repeated attacks of cavalry and infantry, occasionally mixed, but sometimes separate, which were made upon it. In one of these the enemy carried the farm house of La Haye Sainte, as the detachment of the light battalion of the German Legion, which occupied it, had expended all its ammunition, and the enemy occupied the only communication there was with them.

The enemy repeatedly charged our infantry with his cavalry, but these attacks were uniformly unsuccessful; and they afforded opportunities to our cavalry to charge, in one of which Lord E. Somerset's brigade, consisting of the Life Guards, the Royal Horse Guards, and 1st dragoon guards, highly distinguished themselves, as did that of Major General Sir William Ponsonby, having taken many prisoners and an eagle.

These attacks were repeated till about seven in the evening, when the enemy made a desperate effort with cavalry and infantry, supported by the fire of artillery, to force our left centre, near the farm of La Haye Sainte, which, after a severe contest, was defeated; and, having observed that the troops retired from this attack in great confusion, and that the march of General Bülow's corps, by Frischermont, upon Planchenois and La Belle Alliance, had begun to take effect, and as I could perceive the fire of his cannon, and as Marshal Prince Blücher had joined in person with a corps of his army to the left of our line by Ohain, I determined to attack the enemy, and immediately advanced the whole line of infantry, supported by the cavalry and artillery. The attack succeeded in every point: the enemy was forced from his positions on the heights, and fled in the utmost confusion, leaving behind him, as far as I could judge, 150 pieces of cannon, with their ammunition, which fell into our hands. I continued the pursuit till long after dark, and then discontinued it only on account of the fatigue of our troops, who had been engaged during twelve hours, and because I found myself on the same road with Marshal Blücher, who assured me of his intention to follow the enemy throughout the night. He has sent me word this morning that he had taken 60 pieces of cannon belonging to the Imperial Guard, and several carriages, baggage, &c., belonging to Buonaparte, in Genappe.

I propose to move this morning upon Nivelles, and not to discontinue my operations.

Your Lordship will observe that such a desperate action could not be fought, and such advantages could not be gained, without great loss; and I am sorry to add that ours has been immense. In Lieutenant General Sir Thomas Picton His Majesty has sustained the loss of an officer who has frequently distinguished himself in his service, and he fell gloriously leading his division to a charge with bayonets, by which one of the most serious attacks made by the enemy on our position was repulsed, The Earl of Uxbridge, after having successfully got through this arduous day, received a wound by almost the last shot fired, which will, I am afraid, deprive His Majesty for some time of his services

His Royal Highness the Prince of Orange distinguished himself by his gallantry and conduct, till he received a wound from a musket ball through the shoulder, which obliged him to quit the field.

It gives me the greatest satisfaction to assure your Lordship that the army never, upon any occasion, conducted itself better. The division of Guards, under Lieutenant General Cooke, who is severely wounded, Major General Maitland, and Major General Byng, set an example which was followed by all; and there is no officer nor description of troops that did not behave well.

I must, however, particularly mention, for His Royal Highness's approbation, Lieutenant General Sir H. Clinton, Major General Adam, Lieutenant General Charles Baron Alten, severely wounded, Major General Sir Colin Halbet, severely wounded;, Colonel Ompteda, commanding a brigade of the 4th division; Major General Sir James Kempt and Sir Denis Pack, Major General Lambert, Major General Lord E. Somerset; Major General Sir W. Ponsonby; Major General Sir C. Grant, and Major General Sir H. Vivian, Major General Sir O. Vandeleur; Major General Count Dornberg.

I am also particularly indebted to General Lord Hill for his assistance and conduct upon this as upon all former occasions .

The artillery and engineer departments were conducted much to my satisfaction by Colonel Sir G. Wood and Col. Smyth; and I had every reason to be satisfied with the conduct of the Adjt General, Major Gen Barnes, who was wounded, and of the Quarter Master General, Col Delancy, who was killed by a cannon shot in the middle of the action. This officer is a serious loss to His Majesty's service, and to me at this moment. I was likewise much indebted to the assistance of Lieutenant Colonel Lord Fitzroy Somerset, who was severely wounded, and of the officers composing my personal staff, who have suffered severely in this action. Lieutenant Colonel the Honourable Sir Alexander Gordon who has died of his wounds was a most promising officer, and is a serious loss to His Majesty's Service.

General Kruse, of the Nassau service, likewise conducted himself to my satisfaction, as did General Trip, commanding the heavy brigade of cavalry, and General Vanhope, commanding a Brigade of infantry in the service of the King of the Netherlands.

General Pozzo di Borgo, General Baron Vincent, General Muffling, and General Alvoa, were in the field during the action, and rendered me every assistance in their power. Baron Vincent is wounded, but I hope not severely; and General Pozzo di Borgo received a contusion.

I should not do justice to my feelings or to Marshal Blücher and the Prussian army, if I did not attribute the successful result of this arduous day, to the cordial and timely assistance I received from them. The operation of General Bülow upon th[e] enemy's flank, was a most decisive one; and even if I had not found myself in a situation to make the attack, which produced the final result, it would have forced the enemy to retire if his attacks should have failed, and would have prevented him from taking advantage of them if they should unfortunately have succeeded.

I send with this despatch, two eagles, taken by the troops in this action, which Major Percy will have the honour of laying at the feet of His Royal Highness.

I beg leave to recommend him to your Lordship's protection. I have the honour, &c,

WELLINGTON

P.S. Since writing the above, I have received a report that Major General Sir William Ponsonby is killed; and, in announcing this intelligence to your Lordship, I have to add the expression of my grief for the fate of an officer who had already rendered very brilliant and important services, and was an ornament to his profession.

2nd P.S. I have not yet got the returns of killed and wounded, but I enclose a list of officers killed and wounded on the two days, as far as the same can be made out without the returns; and I am very happy to add, that Colonel de Lancey is not dead, and that strong hopes of his recovery are entertained.

AFTERMATH

THE HUNDRED DAYS SHOOK EUROPE TO ITS CORE. It will always stand as an example of a supreme moment of crisis when the course of history hung in the balance. However, the status quo prevailed, albeit by the narrowest of margins. Napoleon was defeated and imprisoned, never to play another part on the world stage – at least for the rest of his life. The Bourbons were restored to the Tuileries Palace and the great powers resumed the work of rebuilding Europe after decades of war that had obliterated centuries-old certainties.

Had more vindictive voices prevailed, Waterloo could have marked a radical shift in allied policy towards France. The Prussians never forgot nor forgave Napoleon and France for humbling their army so comprehensively in 1806. They were restrained by the British, who – as has

been their policy for centuries – believed the best solution for Europe was a balance of power on the Continent. The British did not wish to simply swap French hegemony for that of Prussia or Russia.

At the Congress of Vienna, the British wanted to give France's new monarchy the best possible chance. Some colonies were forfeited but swingeing territorial confiscations were avoided. France would start the new post-war era as an important European power, not a defeated, penalized husk. If the French people associated the restored monarchy with humiliation and economic failure, then the embers of revolutionary fervour could so easily be fanned back into flame. It is to Wellington's great credit that his genius on the battlefield was matched by a subtlety and far-sightedness in diplomacy. He and the

Below: French onlookers witness the review of British troops by the Duke of Wellington in Montmartre, Paris, on 21 October 1815. The French monarchy under Louis XVIII has been restored and there will be no major Europe-wide conflict for the next century.

Overleaf: The Duke of Wellington hosts the Waterloo banquet at his home, Apsley House in London, in 1836. Some but not all of his generals have died, and a few will live on to celebrate the final dinner held in 1852, three months before Wellington's death and 37 years after Waterloo.

ROBERT JENKINSON, 2ND EARL OF LIVERPOOL
(1770–1828)

Wellington owed a great deal to Lord Liverpool. The first thing the politician did when he became British Secretary for War and the Colonies in 1809 was to get Cabinet support for Wellington's force in Portugal. Between 1809 and 1811, annual expenditure on the Peninsular campaign rose from £3 million to £9 million pounds. Lord Liverpool was prime minister from 1812 to 1827. Although his tenure was the longest in British history, he is one of the least-known leaders. A contemporary summed him us as "a meek spirit, too meek for a premier but he could judge with calmness and correctness on the data submitted to him, though perhaps not very quickly".

British Foreign Secretary, Lord Castlereagh, ably assisted by the brilliantly resourceful French Foreign Minister, Talleyrand, slowly convinced the other delegates that vengeance would simply ensure continued conflict.

Many others believed that France must pay for the awful violence that had swirled across Europe for a generation. The British prime minister, Lord Liverpool, favoured a harsh settlement. The Prussians wanted the French provinces of Alsace and Lorraine. Despite this, Talleyrand, Wellington and Castlereagh had skilfully manoeuvred France into an important position at the Congress. The return of Napoleon in the spring of 1815 and the anger it provoked among the allies undid some of this hard work, but many of the provisions had been agreed upon before Napoleon had briefly returned to power. Although some further penalties were imposed after Waterloo, the settlement remained remarkably lenient on France, which returned to her borders as they were at the time of the French Revolution. An army of occupation numbering 150,000, not thought necessary before the Hundred Days, was to be stationed in France and paid for by the French. This would protect France's neighbours from the threat of future invasion and ensure

the payment of reparations totalling 700 million francs, the price of Napoleon's desperate gamble. The peace treaty was signed on 20 November 1815.

The Congress of Vienna and its attendant treaties did not simply deal with how to punish France. They reordered the rest of Europe and its colonies around the world. Britain was able to keep many of the choice territories it had wrestled off competitors during the war. Russia absorbed most of Poland, and Prussia tightened its grip on northern and eastern Germany.

Castlereagh, just like the peacemakers following the awful wars of the twentieth century, wanted to find a way to allow the great powers of Europe to resolve their differences without resorting to the kind of titanic warfare that had proved so destructive to lives, property and to the social fabric that he and his fellow diplomats prized so highly. The result was an idea rather than an institution. The Concert of Europe was a name given to a strategic approach by Europe's leaders. Whenever there was a crisis or dispute, a

Below: A rosette from a French shako, a soldier's headgear, found on the Waterloo battlefield. The rosette is a circular red, white and blue tricolour made of crimped cotton.

THE LAST WATERLOO BANQUET
18 JUNE 1852

Every year, on Waterloo day – 18 June – Wellington hosted a Waterloo banquet at his Piccadilly residence, Apsley House, known as "Number 1 London". The last dinner was held three months before Wellington's death in 1852, 37 years after his victory at Waterloo. He proposed a toast to each of the dwindling number of his fellow commanders in the battle. At the age of 83, the duke was recognized wherever he went as a national hero. There was one famous exception when a man met him walking his dog in Hyde Park. "Mr Jones, I believe?" said the man. "If you believe that," the duke fired back, "you'll believe anything."

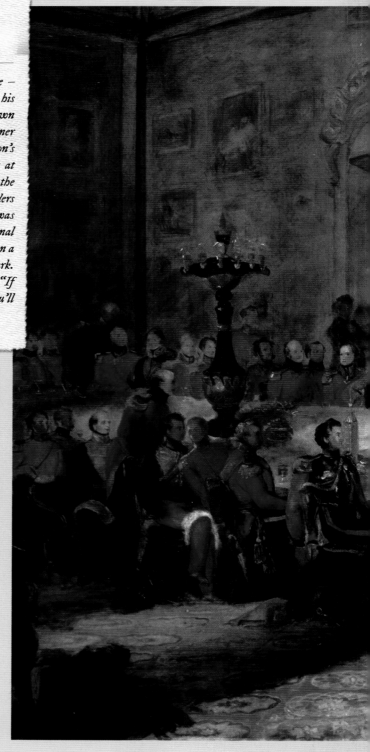

summit would be held. Europe's politicians would gather to trade concessions and all-out war would be avoided. This system lasted, albeit imperfectly, for decades. One of the most famous gatherings was the London conference in 1832, at which the great powers decided on the shape and nature of an independent Greece.

Europe would see several wars over the next century, but none was on the scale of the Revolutionary and Napoleonic Wars. As memories of these bitter and destructive conflicts faded, and new international rivalries burned bright, Europe's statesmen allowed another war to tear the continent apart in 1914. Not only were millions of men killed and injured in this new war, it also proved a cataclysm for the ruling class of Europe as revolutions followed in its wake. It was upheaval of just the sort that the conservative reformers, Castlereagh and his contemporaries, had sought to stave off.

Some of those who fought during The Hundred Days would never see another

Below: The village of Waterloo with travellers purchasing relics found on the field of battle. A Prussian soldier and a local woman offer souvenirs to a mounted hussar, a highlander and some tourists on a coach from Brussels. The artist, George Jones, visited Waterloo immediately after the battle and painted this eyewitness record of the market in souvenirs, most of them stripped from the dead on the field.

battlefield, while others were just at the start of long careers. Napoleon Bonaparte died six years later on St Helena. There is debate over whether he was poisoned or whether it was cancer that killed him. Certainly, specialists at the FBI have found suspiciously high concentrations of arsenic in a hair sample. He breathed his last on 5 May 1821, aged 51. In delirium at the end he talked of "Elysium" where he would compare victories with Scipio, Hannibal, Caesar and Frederick. "There will be pleasure", he insisted, "in that." Napoleon would continue to make his enemies quake even in death. The British, perhaps foolishly, allowed his body to be repatriated to be buried in Paris on 5 December 1840. With all the pomp that could be mustered, accompanied by his ageing veterans, the emperor's coffin was drawn through the packed streets as crowds roared and a powerful nationalism stirred.

Wellington became a figure on the national stage for which there is almost no equal in British history. Not only was he Europe's greatest military commander, but he rapidly became one of the most important politicians – if not the most important politician – in the King's cabinet. He was made Commander in Chief of the British Army in 1827 and, reluctantly, accepted the office of prime minister the following year. He felt obliged to pass Catholic emancipation to avoid a civil war in Ireland but this only seemed to encourage the calls for far-reaching political reform. Wellington refused to countenance further changes to the British constitution and was replaced by a reformist administration. He continued at the centre of public life until shortly before his death in 1852, aged 83. One and a half million people lined the streets as his funeral cortege passed through London on its way to St Paul's Cathedral.

Wellington's ally Blücher died in 1819 on his Silesian estates. Napoleon's right-hand man, the brilliant but flawed Marshal Ney, finally proved he was mortal after all when he was executed by firing squad in December 1815. Some younger men would go on to play vital roles in subsequent wars. Fitzroy Somerset was on Wellington's staff and lost his arm at Waterloo. He would command British forces in the Crimea, where he died a broken man after the campaign became mired in stalemate. Prince Wilhelm, heir to the Hohenzollern Prussian throne, commanded a Guards battalion at Waterloo; as king, he would later command Prussian forces against the Austrians and French from 1866 to 1871, when Prussia cemented her domination of central Europe.

Waterloo decisively ended an era of total war on the continent of Europe. No one doubted its importance at the time. Tourism began almost immediately as citizens of Brussels flooded south to look at the war-torn field. British and French visitors soon followed. For the last time in the history of Western Europe, its fate had been decided in one day on a small battlefield, which a visitor could absorb – almost – from a single spot. Sightseers flocked, as thousands still do, to the place where their continent's fate had been thrashed out, and where two of history's greatest commanders had fought each other in a close-run battle in which the margin of victory was thin but the impact total.

The battle is a looming presence throughout the works of Byron, Thackeray, Victor Hugo and Hardy. Towns, stations, bridges and monuments named after the battle are still to be found around the world as British settlers built new worlds while saluting the greatest achievements of the old. The very word "Waterloo" has become a widely used synonym for a final, decisive event. Perhaps the battle's mystique endures in an age of massive military expenditure, hardware, robotics and systems, because the day on which it occurred was one when history hung in the balance. It was a day on which decisions taken by commanders, the grit and initiative of frontline infantry and cavalrymen, blind luck and bad weather shaped the future of the world.

LETTER TO THE DUKE OF WELLINGTON
25 AUGUST 1815

Letter written in late August 1815 from a French school mistress in Montmartre, Paris, imploring Wellington, whom she address as "Monsieur le Duc", to withdraw his men who have been billeting at her property since July. There is a note at the top in Wellington's hand asking an aide to "Get Colonel Scovell to go and see this woman and arrange that the officers should quit her house. Let them know however that I am very much satisfied with them."

Monsieur le Duc

I run a pension for young ladies in a house of that I own, situated in the lower part of Montmartre outside the city fortifications. As a consequence I would like to beg J.E. to grant this house an exemption from military lodgings.

For the past 28 days, two captains of the 12th regiment of the English infantry, their soldiers and their horses, have been imposed upon me as lodgers in my house. I am happy to tell J.E. that these gentlemen were very well behaved; however, I cannot help but add that, even if their comportment was faultless, their stay has been for my household a terrible calamity due to the impropriety of seeing military men in an educational establishment for young girls. One wouldn't be shocked if I could make public the account that the decency and the restraint that distinguishes the officers that I have accommodated deserves; J.E. knows very well that I can't and that I am a victim of appearances.

If the very existence of my family were not dependent on that of my pension, I would not disturb J.E. with my request; but at risk of seeing the complete ruin of an establishment that has already suffered the tragedies of France, I find myself obliged to beg J.E. to grant me the object of my request.

The mercy that I dare to hope J.E. might show me will only intensify the gratitude felt by this French heart who trusts in his kindness.

In this sentiment, Monsieur le Duc, I have the honour, with respect of J.E.

Your very humble servant

..., school mistress

Montmartre, 25 August 1815

Cpt Colonel Scovill
to go & see the
woman & arrange
that the Officers
Monsieur le Duc
should quit her house
to other house
however that I am

Very much satisfied
North Paris

Je tiens un pensionnat de jeunes demoiselles dans une maison qui m'appartient, et qui est située au bas de Montmartre, hors de l'enceinte des fortifications : je viens en conséquence supplier V. E. d'accorder à cette maison l'exemption de logements militaires.

Depuis 28 jours, deux capitaines du 12ᵉ régiment d'infanterie anglaise, 4 soldats et 4 chevaux, ont été d'autorité logés dans ma maison. Je me plais à dire à V. E. que ces messieurs s'y très bien comportés; cependant je ne puis m'empêcher d'ajouter que, même en y tenant une conduite parfaite, leur séjour a été pour ma maison une véritable calamité, par l'inconvenance dont il est de voir des militaires dans une maison d'éducation de jeunes demoiselles. On n'en serait pas choqué, si je pouvais rendre public le témoignage que méritent la décence et la retenue qui distinguent messrs les officiers que j'ai logés : V. E. sait bien que je ne le peux pas et je suis victime des apparences.

Si l'existence de ma famille ne tenait pas à celle de mon pensionnat, je n'importunerais pas V. E. de ma réclamation; mais sous peine de voir ruiner tout-à-fait un établissement qui a déjà tant souffert des malheurs de la France, je me trouve forcée de supplier V. E. de m'accorder l'objet de ma demande.

Cette grâce que j'ose espérer de V. E. augmentera la reconnaissance dont est déjà pénétré un cœur français qui se confie à sa bonté.

Dans ces sentiments, Monsieur le Duc, j'ai l'honneur avec respect de V. E.

La très humble servante
Enᵉ Pinon, institutrice

Montmartre ce 25 août 1815

THE DUKE OF WELLINGTON
20 MARCH 1816

Wellington notifies Major James Gunthorpe, who was Brigade-Major of General Sir Peregrine Maitland's 1st British Brigade of Guards at Waterloo, that he will be awarded the Waterloo medal. It was the first campaign medal ever awarded by the British Army to everyone irrespective of rank.

Paris, March 20 1816

Sir,

The Prince Regent having been graciously pleased, in the Name and on Behalf of His Majesty, to command that a Medal should be struck for the Officers, and Men, who fought at the Battle of Waterloo, I have the honor to forward the one destined for you
and to be
Sir,
Your obedient humble Servant
Wellington

To Major James Gunthorpe
1ˢᵗ Guards

Paris, March 20th 1816.

Sir,

The Prince Regent having been graciously pleased, in the Name and on the Behalf of His Majesty, to command that a Medal should be struck for the Officers, and Men, who fought at the Battle of Waterloo, I have the honor to forward the one destined for you

and to be

Sir,

Your obedient humble Servant,

Wellington

To Major James Sunthorpe
1st Guards

INDEX

CREDITS

The publisher would like to thank the following sources for their kind permission to reproduce the pictures in this book.

Unless otherwise stated below, images © The National Army Museum, London.

2. BI/English Heritage Photo Library, 9. BI/Chateau de Versailles, France, 10. Photo © RMN-Grand Palais,11. The Art Archive/Musée du Château de Versailles/Gianni Dagli Orti, 12. BI/Apsley House, The Wellington Museum, London, UK, 14-15. BI/State Museum Tsarskoye Selo, St. Petersburg, 16. BI/Chateau de Versailles, France, 17. BI/Photo © Christie's Images, 18. BI/Apsley House, The Wellington Museum, London, UK, 19. BI/Musee de l'Armee, Brussels, Belgium/Patrick Lorette, 23. Service historique de la Défence, department de l'Armée de terre, Paris, 24. Photo © RMN-Grand Palais, 25. & 26. (top) BI/Château de Versailles, France, 26-27. The National Gallery, UK, 29. BI/Château de Versailles, France, 33. BI/Private Collection/The Stapleton Collection, 40. National Gallery of Victoria, Melbourne, Australia, 43. & 45 (bottom) BI/© Historic England, 50-51. Museums Sheffield, 51 (top) BI/The Bowes Museum, Barnard Castle, County Durham, UK, 54. Museums Sheffield, 55. The Art Archive/Bibliothèque Nationale Paris, 60-61. The National Archives of the UK, Kew, 62. BI/

Apsley House, The Wellington Museum, London, UK, 69. (bottom) BI/Private Collection, 70-71. BI/ Leeds Museums and Galleries, 80-81. BI/Dahesh Museum of Art, New York, USA, 84-85. BI/Apsley House, The Wellington Museum, London, UK, 91. BI/Interfoto/Alamy, 92-93. The Art Archive/CCI, 94-95. Photo Scala, Florence/bpk, 95. BI/Private Collection/© Look and Learn, 98-99. & 102-103. AKG-Images, 106-107. BI/English Heritage Photo Library & 108. (top), 110-111. Tim Koster, Cultural Heritage Agency of the Netherlands Rijswijk/Amersfoort, 120. AKG-Images, 121. BI/Yale Center for British Art, Paul Mellon Collection, USA, 125. & 137. BI/Photo © Bonhams, London, UK, 138. (top) Topfoto/British Library, 138. (top right) AKG-Images, 139. (bottom) BI/Private Collection, 140. (top) BI/The Crown Estate, 141. BI/© Lady Lever Art Gallery, National Museums Liverpool, 149. (top)) BI/National Trust Photographic Library/Angelo Hornak, 150-151. BI/Private Collection/Photo, 155 & 157. The National Archives of the UK, Kew

BI = Bridgeman Images

Every effort has been made to acknowledge correctly and contact the source and/or copyright holder of each picture and Carlton Books Limited apologises for any unintentional errors or omissions, which will be corrected in future editions of this book.